Revolution in Guinea
An African People's struggle

Selected texts by **Amilcar Cabral**

SELECTED TEXTS BY
AMILCAR CABRAL

REVOLUTION IN GUINEA

AN AFRICAN PEOPLE'S STRUGGLE

STAGE 1

Printed in Great Britain by Love & Malcomson Limited, Brighton Road, Redhill, Surrey.

SBN 85035 002 6 Cloth edition
85035 003 4 Paperback

Stage 1, 21 Theobalds Road, London WC1, England

Contents

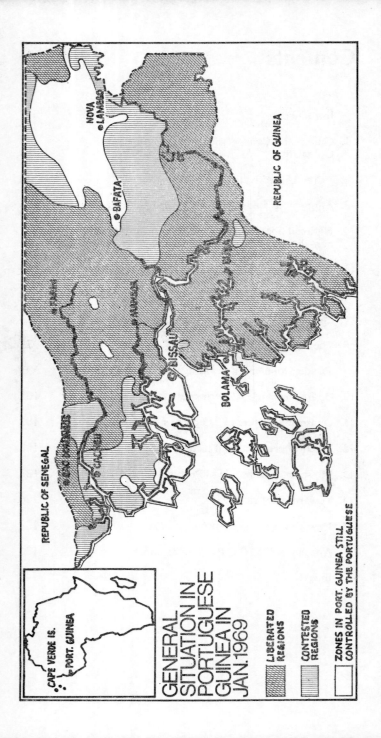

GENERAL SITUATION IN PORTUGUESE GUINEA IN JAN.1969

LIBERATED REGIONS

CONTESTED REGIONS

ZONES IN PORT. GUINEA STILL CONTROLLED BY THE PORTUGUESE

CAPE VERDE IS.

PORT. GUINEA

REPUBLIC OF SENEGAL

REPUBLIC OF GUINEA

NOVA LAMEGO

BAFATA

BISSAU

BOLAMA

CACHEU

SÃO DOMINGOS

Introduction

The people of 'Portuguese' Guinea took up arms to free their country from colonial domination in 1963, under the leadership of the Partido Africano da Independencia da Guiné e Cabo Verde (PAIGC). Today, in spite of a Portuguese military presence even stronger, in proportion to the populations involved, than the United States forces in Vietnam, the PAIGC controls over two-thirds of Guinea and, while continuing and extending the armed struggle, is completely transforming the life of the people within the liberated areas.

The development and continued success of this struggle is obviously not fortuitous. The conditions for popular armed struggle may exist independently of any movement and the struggle may even break out spontaneously; but it cannot grow and extend over six years without thorough organisation and clear political leadership. The development of the struggle in Guinea has been documented both in books and in films: two recent books in particular, Gérard Chaliand's *Armed Struggle in Africa*₁ and Basil Davidson's *The Liberation of Guiné*₂ indicate the importance of the political analysis and action underlying the military success.

Amilcar Cabral, the founder and present Secretary-General of the PAIGC, and the small group which formed the original core of the Party, saw the necessity of freeing their country from Portuguese colonial domination. The experiences of other liberation movements, the growth of neo-colonialism in newly 'independent' African countries, and above all the development of the movement within Guinea itself made clear the necessity of a true socialist revolution if any real change was to be made in Guinea. Finally, the savage Portuguese repression of the PAIGC's early peaceful actions quickly showed the inevitability of armed struggle. But Guinea had none of the elements on which revolution in Europe and Asia had been based. There was no large proletariat, no developed working class, no large peasant mass deprived of land (colonial exploitation in Guinea being carried out through the price mechanism rather than by land ownership). A successful revolutionary strategy for Guinea could not be based on any wholesale adoption of other revolutionary experiences—what was needed was a strategy based on African conditions, on the conditions within Guinea itself.

From 1952 to 1954, Amilcar Cabral had visited every corner of his country, preparing an agricultural census for the colonial administration, and in the process acquiring a detailed knowledge of his own people and their situation. This knowledge provided the basis for the PAIGC's revolutionary strategy. Starting from a detailed analysis of the social structure of the different tribal groups section 5), Cabral weighed up the revolutionary potential of each group and the PAIGC's long, patient process of clandestine political preparation began on this basis in 1959. The details of this process emerge in Cabral's declaration to the United Nations (section 2) and in the *Tricontinental* interviews (sections 12 and 14): extracts from a general Party directive of 1965 (section 7) show the clear, down-to-earth terms in which the political aims are put into practice. This careful political preparation for the armed struggle is clearly paralleled by the similar process described in Wilfred Burchett's book *Vietnam will Win*$_3$.

Cabral's political analysis does, however, go beyond the confines of Guinea itself. In his speech to the Tricontinental Conference in Havana in 1966 (section 8) he makes a contribution of major importance to revolutionary theory. While accepting the central role of class struggle at a given historical stage, he goes further to examine the determining elements of class struggle and concludes that the true motive force of history is the mode of production, thus "avoiding for some human groups in our countries . . . the sad position of being peoples without history". Proceeding with a clear analysis of imperialism in its various forms, he finally tackles the problem of the contradictory role of the revolutionary bourgeoisie in the liberation struggles of underdeveloped countries. This section, perhaps more than any other, clearly shows Cabral's importance as a revolutionary thinker.

The importance of the PAIGC's struggle to the revolutionary movement in Africa is out of all proportion to the physical size of Guinea (15,500 square miles, roughly the size of Switzerland or half the size of Maine; 800,000 inhabitants, the approximate population of Liverpool or San Francisco city). Militarily, politically and economically, the Portuguese are clearly losing the war, and indeed there can be little doubt that they would have abandoned Guinea long ago if it were not for the seriously adverse propaganda effect that such an admission of defeat would have in their other colonies of Angola and Mozambique, where the economic reasons for maintaining their domination are much stronger. The final victory of the PAIGC's struggle, which can only be a matter of time, will significantly influence the development of the struggle in Southern Africa, both in Portugal's other colonies of Angola and Mozambique and against the fascist, racist regimes of South Africa and Rhodesia and the imperialist powers backing these regimes.

To revolutionary movements throughout the world, including, and perhaps particularly those in Europe, the struggle in Guinea is of prime importance as an outstanding illustration of the need to study one's own concrete conditions and to make the revolution according to these conditions, rather than relying on the experience of others, valuable as this may be.

This book has not been planned to give a detailed, factual account of the development of the struggle in Guinea—that has been done elsewhere, particularly in the two books mentioned above. While the development of the struggle inevitably emerges in the text, the purpose is to present the writings of an outstanding revolutionary thinker. Faced with the difficulty of choosing what to include, it was finally decided to present as full a range as possible of texts originally addressed to a wide variety of audiences. These have been cut only to avoid as much repetition as possible. To simplify the text, 'Portuguese' Guinea has been called simply Guinea throughout.

Thanks are due to Editions François Maspéro for permission to use the texts in *Partisans* numbers 7 and 26/27 which appear in sections 1 and 8; to *Pensamiento Critico,* Havana, for the text of section 5 and their fuller version of the text of section 8; to Basil Davidson for his help and advice; to many other friends who have helped in different ways in the preparation of this collection; and above all to the people of Guinea and the PAIGC, without whom this book would not have been possible.

Any lack of clarity or inaccuracy in the text must be attributed to the translator and editor, but it is hoped that this collection will do justice to the thought of Amilcar Cabral and at the same time help to stimulate analysis of a similar clarity, and action of a similar strength, among revolutionaries wherever they may be.

Richard Handyside *editor and translator*

1) François Maspéro, Paris, 1967/Monthly Review Press 1969
2) Penguin Books, London, 1969
3) Guardian, New York/Monthly Review Press, 1968

Guinea and Cabo Verde against Portuguese Colonialism

Speech made at the 3rd Conference of the African Peoples held in Cairo, March 25-31, 1961

The absurdity of our situation

The situation of our peoples, like that of the other peoples dominated by Portugal, seems absurd. The fundamental rights of man, essential freedoms, respect for human dignity —all these are unknown in our country. While the colonial powers in general accept the principle of self-determination of peoples and seek, each in its own way, to resolve the conflicts which oppose them to the people they dominate, the Portuguese government obstinately maintains its domination and exploitation of 15 million human beings, of whom 12 million are African. While the overwhelming majority of the African peoples, in spite of the contradictions and difficulties which they face, are beginning the peaceful construction of progress, our peoples, because of the Portuguese colonialists, are obliged to go on living in the most extreme misery, ignorance and fear.

The Portuguese colonialists try, in vain, to convince the world that they have no colonies and that our African countries are 'provinces of Portugal'. The Portuguese are pursuing, arresting, torturing, killing, massacring, launching a colonial war in Angola and feverishly preparing for a new war in Guinea and Cabo Verde.

And yet the situation imposed on our peoples by the Portuguese colonialists is not as absurd as one might think. Obviously violence and lies have been, and still are, the main weapons of any colonialism. But when the colonising country has a fascist government, when the people of that country are largely illiterate, and neither know nor enjoy the fundamental human rights and have a very low standard of living in their own country; when furthermore the economy of the metropolis is under-developed, as is the case in Portugal, then violence and lies reach an unparalleled height, and lack of respect for the African people knows no limits.

In the last thirty-five years, this situation has become considerably worse. Caricatures of the Portuguese economic and political systems, new forms of oppression and repression have been brought into action, and our people have begun to live in a veritable state of siege. For a long time, the fascist-colonial government of Portugal succeeded, by combining silence, cynicism and hypocrisy, in preventing world opinion from knowing the crimes of the Portuguese colonialists. It must not be forgotten that the temporary success of this policy of silence was largely due to the complicity and assistance of certain economic powers in other countries, which had and still have the strongest interest in 'conserving' the Portuguese colonies.

We are no longer concerned here with unmasking the Portuguese colonialists, whose monstrous behaviour is today evident to the whole world. We wish only to recall that the denunciation of the Portuguese colonial crime was the work of the peoples of the Portuguese colonies themselves, as the result of a systematic revolutionary plan carried out by African patriots in the international field. Faced with the strongest resistance, and even hostility, of some Western circles, these African patriots, aware of the strategic necessity of isolating the Portuguese colonialists even from their own allies, spared no efforts to accomplish this historic mission.

The certainty of our total victory against Portuguese colonialism, on an international level, is today evident. It was consecrated by the vote of the United Nations General Assembly on December 14th, 1960, which confirmed by an overwhelming majority the resolution of the Trusteeship Council demanding information from Portugal about the situation of the peoples which it dominated. Even taking into account the formal, moral character of this victory, it represents a great step forward in our liberation struggle, for we have managed to isolate our enemy.

No power can shake us from our determination, nor prevent the rapid and total elimination of Portuguese domination in our countries.

However, to free themselves from foreign domination is not the only desire of our peoples. They have learned by experience under colonial oppression that the exploitation of man by man is the biggest obstacle in the way of the development and progress of a people beyond national liberation. They are determined to take an active part in the building of a new Africa, truly independent and progressive, founded on work and justice, in which the creative power of our people which has been stifled for centuries will find its truest and most constructive expression.

We are conscious of the fact that our victory will not be easy. We have many centuries' experience of the nature of our enemy and of its particular characteristics in relation to the other colonial powers. Although it is isolated, we should not forget that it still has at its disposal forces of destruction far superior to our own and that, overtly or covertly, it is aided and supported by other forces hostile to the freedom and progress of the peoples of Africa.

The essential characteristics of our time. The death-throes of imperialism. The case of Portugal.

Imperialism, or the monopolistic stage of capitalism, has been unable to escape from its own contradictions; by use of force the victorious powers of the first world war set about a new sharing-out of the world, characterised mainly by the reinforcement of the colonial position of England and France and by the exclusion of Germany from direct exploitation of so-called backward peoples and countries.

In the final phase of this conflict, the victory of the October Revolution and the definitive implantation of socialism on one sixth of the world's surface came as the first major blow to imperialism.

Deprived of sources of raw materials and surplus profits, German financial capital, in alliance with Italian and Japanese capital, tried to solve the problem by taking the shortest road—the colonisation of their own European neighbours. The second world war was the result of the antagonisms which characterise the development of imperialism, but it came to influence very decisively the destiny of the other peoples of the world, particularly those of Africa.

At the same time as the strengthening of the socialist camp, another essential characteristic of our time, came the awakening of the dependent peoples for the liberation struggle and the final phase of the elimination of imperialism had thus begun. While the final resolution of this new conflict may take a shorter or a longer time, there can be no doubt that, even more than the class struggle in the capitalist countries and the antagonism between these countries and the socialist world, the liberation struggle of the colonial peoples is the essential characteristic, and we would say the prime motive force, of the advance of history in our times: and it is to this struggle, to this conflict on three continents that our national liberation struggle against Portuguese colonialism is linked.

Faced with the power of the main imperialist nations, one is forced to wonder how it was possible for Portugal, an underdeveloped and backward country, to retain its colonies in spite of the redistribution to which the world was subjected. Portuguese colonialism managed to survive despite the sharing-out of Africa made by the imperialist powers at the end of the 19th century because England supported the ambitions of Portugal which, since the treaty of Metwen in 1703 had become a semi-colony of England. England had every interest in using the Portuguese colonies, not only to exploit their economic resources, but also to occupy them as support bases on the route to the Orient, and thus to maintain absolute domination in the Indian Ocean. To counter the greed of the other colonialist powers and to defend its interests in the Portuguese colonies, England found the best solution: it defended the 'rights' of its semi-colony. That is why, for example, Portugal granted to a private enterprise controlled by English interests sovereign rights over an area covering 17% of the total territory of Mozambique.

In fact Portugal has been no more than the sometimes envious guardian of the human and material resources of our countries, at the service of world imperialism. That is the real reason for the survival of Portuguese colonialism in Africa, and for the possible prolonging of our struggle. Thus to a greater extent than the presence of other powers in Africa, the presence of Portugal has been, and still is dependent on the presence of other colonising powers, mainly England.

The African revolution. Victories and failures. The evolution of Africa.

It is sufficient to look at the political map of present-day Africa to recognise that the African peoples have already won some great victories. But it is also sufficient to have followed closely the main events in this struggle to recognise that numerous and great mistakes have been made. The year 1960—the year of Africa—is rich in examples of both the victories and the failures of the liberation struggle of the African peoples.

Once again, the heroic people of Algeria have accelerated the advance of history. Several peoples have seen their aspirations confounded by a nominal independence. The peoples of South Africa, like those of our own countries, of Angola, Mozambique and the other Portuguese colonies, continue to be subjected to the most violent exploitation and the most barbarous colonial repression. The practice of African solidarity reveals some hesitation and even improvisation which our enemies have been able to exploit in their favour. Perhaps the most important, and certainly the most dramatic of the failures (and also of the errors) is the case of the Congo, tragically crowned by the assassination of Patrice Lumumba. In reality these failures and errors have taught us many important things. One can say that the year 1960, and more particularly the Congo drama, has given back to the African his human dimensions.

Victories or failures, we must not forget that not one of our enemies has been really and totally conquered and driven out of Africa. The fascist-colonialist Portuguese are continuing to massacre our peoples in Guinea, Angola and Mozambique; the fascist-racists of South Africa are daily strengthening their hateful apparatus of apartheid; the Belgian colonialists have returned to the Congo from which they had been driven out; the British imperialists and colonialists are using every twist of imagination and cynicism in an attempt to maintain their complete domination over East Africa and their economic domination of the West African colonies; the French imperialists and colonialists are killing defenceless people in Algeria, exploding atomic bombs on African soil, trying to create a new geographical, historical and technical absurdity—the 'French province' of the Sahara—and increasing their economic domination over some of our African peoples; the American imperialists are emerging from the shadows and, astonished by the weakness of their partners, are seeking to replace them everywhere, with varying degrees of sublety.

Our enemies are determined to strike mortal blows against us and to turn our victories into defeats. To attain this goal, they use the most suitable instrument—African traitors. And here is a reality that is made more evident by our struggle: in spite of their armed forces, the imperialists cannot do without traitors; traditional chiefs and bandits in the times of slavery and of the wars of colonial conquest, gendarmes, various agents and mercenary soldiers during the golden age of colonialism, self-styled heads of state and ministers in the present time of neo-colonialism. The enemies of the African peoples are powerful and cunning and can always count on a few faithful lackeys in our country, since quislings are not a European privilege.

However, if we want to neutralise the delaying actions carried out by our enemies and their lackeys, we must strengthen the methods of action and the vigilance of the African revolution. Let us be precise: for us, African revolution means the transformation of our present life in the direction of progress. The prerequisite for this is the elimination of foreign economic domination, on which every other type of domination is dependent. Our vigilance means the rigorous selection of friends, a constant watch and struggle against enemies (both internal and external) and the neutralisation or elimination of all factors opposing progress.

At present the first difficulty—that of winning political autonomy—has already been overcome, despite the remnant of a few zones of classical colonialism whose days are numbered; the greatest difficulties concern the winning of economic independence, the struggle against neo-colonialism. The positive balance-sheet of the year 1960 cannot make us forget the reality of a crisis in the African revolution which, far from being a mere growing pain, is a crisis of knowledge. In several cases, the practice of the liberation struggle and its future perspectives not only lack a theoretical basis, but are also to a greater or lesser degree remote from the concrete reality around them. Local experiences in the conquest of national independence, national unity and the bases for progress have been or are being forgotten.

Our fundamental problem now is to resolve the main contradictions between the interests of our peoples and the interests of the Portuguese colonialists. This means rapid and total elimination of Portuguese domination in Guinea and Cabo Verde, in a life-or-death struggle. We count on the support and concrete assistance of the African peoples, and especially of neighbouring countries.

While the struggle for national independence is our main concern, we should nevertheless envisage, beyond the liberation struggle, the problem of the future of our peoples, of their economic, social and cultural evolution on the road to progress.

In relation to Africa, we are for fraternal collaboration between the African peoples, against narrow nationalisms which do not serve the true interests of the people. A geographic, historical and even ethnic analysis of Africa shows that new forms of economic, political and social existence are developing on the continent. Through contradictions, and even through conflicts, these new and still embryonic forms will become progressively defined in their structure and perhaps in their originality.

We are for African unity, on a regional or continental scale, inasfar as it is necessary for the progress of the African peoples, and in order to guarantee their security and the continuity of this progress.

Our enemy. Isolation and contradictions. The struggle of the people of Angola and of the other colonies.

Our peoples make a distinction between the fascist-colonial government and the people of Portugal: they are not fighting against the Portuguese people. However, the objective situation of the large popular masses in Portugal, oppressed and exploited by the ruling classes of their country, should make them understand the great advantages for them which will flow from the victory of the African peoples over Portuguese colonialism.

It is the educated circles in Portugal, and especially the progressive democrats, who have the task of helping the Portuguese people to destroy the virulent remains of the colonialist, enslaving ideology which in general determines their negative attitude towards the just struggles of the African peoples. To do this, however, these educated circles must also overcome their own imperialist mentality,

15

composed of prejudice and ill-founded disdain for the value and the real capacity of the African peoples. In fact, Portuguese democrats will remain unable to understand the just claims of our peoples until they become convinced that the theory of 'immaturity for self-government' is false and until they realise that oppression is not and will never be a school of virtue and aptitude.

We must reaffirm clearly that while being opposed to all fascism, our peoples are not fighting Portuguese fascism: we are fighting Portuguese colonialism. The destruction of fascism in Portugal must be the work of the Portuguese people themselves: the destruction of Portuguese colonialism will be the work of our peoples. While the fall of fascism in Portugal might not lead to the end of Portuguese colonialism—and this hypothesis has been put forward by some Portuguese opposition leaders—we are certain that the elimination of Portuguese colonialism will bring about the destruction of Portuguese fascism. Through our liberation struggle we are making an effective contribution towards the defeat of Portuguese fascism and giving the Portuguese people the best possible proof of our solidarity. This factor is a cause of pride to our peoples, who hope for the same solidarity from the Portuguese people, through the strengthening of the struggle against fascism.

If the Portuguese opposition was capable of unity within itself, could accept openly the principle of self-determination and independence for our peoples—as certain sectors of it already have done—and could guide the Portuguese people into direct action against fascism, we would be prepared to envisage an alliance of our forces with the democratic and progressive forces of Portugal, with the aim of simultaneous elimination of Portuguese colonialism and fascism. This common struggle against the same enemy forces would create the basis for friendship and future collaboration to serve the interests of our peoples and those of the Portuguese people.

With regard to the United Nations, despite the resolutions favourable to our struggle which the solidarity of the peoples of Africa and Asia and of the progressive forces of the world have had adopted, that organisation has shown itself incapable of resolving disputes between colonised peoples and the colonial powers.

The hypothesis of a change of position or the decay of Portuguese colonialism is just an opportunistic dream, or the result of a false analysis of the nature of Portuguese colonialism. Thus only one way remains: to prepare ourselves as well as we can to destroy within our countries the main forces of Portuguese colonialism. Our peoples have formed a united front for the struggle against Portuguese colonialism with the peoples of the other Portuguese colonies. The conference of the Nationalist Organisations of the Portuguese Colonies (CONCP) held in Casablanca in April 1961 and the creation of a permanent organisation for the co-ordination of our common struggle have been the most recent manifestations of this unity.

The Portuguese government is conscious of one reality: no power in the world will be able to prevent the total elimination of Portuguese colonialism. The dialectic of colonial repression has proved that today no colonialist aggressor can overcome peoples who are determined to win their freedom.

Conscious of the fact that the liberation of our countries depends mainly on the action of our own peoples, on their unity, their capacity for organisation and preparation for the struggle, we are firmly determined to develop our fight.

The situation of our countries. Prospects for the struggle.

The resistance of the people of Guinea and Cabo Verde has never ceased to manifest itself, in revolts, passive resistance, mass emigration to neighbouring countries, and total refusal to pay the taxes of Portuguese domination. Since the days of slavery, innumerable revolts have expressed the people's hatred for Portuguese domination. Mainly at S.Tiago, S. Antâo and S.Vicente, in demonstrations, strikes and revolts, the people have arisen several times against the masters of the land and against foreign domination. Our struggle is carrying on from there.

In Guinea, after the massacre of Pijiguiti Quay (Bissao, 3 August 1959), in the course of which Portuguese soldiers and civilians shot down dozens of striking Guinean workers, a wave of repression and terror organised and commanded by the PIDE (political police) made the life and the struggle of the Guinean people even harder. At the same time the colonial administration, by increasing the export of rice at the expense of the majority of the Guinean people, managed to create a new weapon of oppression—famine.

Very recently, apart from police and military repression, the colonial administration has been using non-violent tactics— presents, bribes, invitations to Portugal for the 'traditional chiefs', scholarships, special radio broadcasts for the 'natives', fostering dissidence and quarrels between the different ethnic groups—with the aim of winning over part of the population and 'dividing to rule'. The colonial administration has been disconcerted by the firm determination of the Guinean people, after the failure of a few preliminary 'meetings' to justify the Portuguese presence.

To ensure the support of certain powers, the Portuguese government grants extensive facilities to non-Portuguese capital for the colonial exploitation of the natural resources (oil, bauxite, etc.) and the manpower of Guinea. Furthermore, it wants to have NATO military bases installed in Guinea and the Cabo Verde Islands in the hope of strengthening its means of repression.

The Portuguese government is still in the process of drawing up an urgent plan for sending thousands of families of Portuguese settlers to Guinea, in the belief that increasing the European population will slow down the development of our liberation struggle. This while in the Cabo Verde Islands the Portuguese government once again let about 10,000 people die of famine in 1958-1959. The Cabo Verdian population, which in only six years (1942-1947) lost 30,000 to 40,000 inhabitants struck down by famine, is always at the mercy of the so-called 'agricultural crises' and subjected to the 'displacement' of thousands of its children as contracted workers for the Portuguese plantations in other colonies. Unemployment has reached catastrophic heights, particularly in S.Vincente, where hundreds of workers have been sacked by English companies.

The peasants, who constitute the majority of the population —and the totality in the agricultural islands (S.Tiago, S. Antâo, S.Nicolau, Fogo)—live at the mercy of the rains, while the pseudo 'economic development plan' is nothing more than a mystification, a source of enrichment for the colonial authorities.

The massive clandestine emigration to Senegal is clear proof of the desperate situation in which the people of Cabo Verde are forced to live. This situation, which is comparable to that of Guinea, has become virtually insupportable with the accentuation of police repression.

In Guinea, agricultural production, the sole base of the economy, founded on mono-cultivation of ground-nuts, is sinking progressively lower. Thousands of peasants are abandoning their homes and seeking peace and the indispensable necessities of life in neighbouring countries. Thus, thousands of Balantes are entering the Republic of Guinea, while ground-nut growers are settling in the Republic of Senegal.

In the urban areas, where repression is greatest, the work of state and private enterprises has been suspended. Hundreds of workers have been dismissed without justification. Numerous enterprises, above all in the rural areas, have given up their activities altogether, strangled by the monopoly of the CUF (Companhia Uniao Fabril)—the true master of Guinea—or pushed by fear of the consequences of our liberation struggle.

Thus the political situation is becoming more tense each day. Guinea is living today in a state of siege, with all the settlers armed and the indigenous population subject to frequent provocations by the army and the colonial police. To fight the rising tide of our liberation struggle, the Portuguese colonialists are constantly reinforcing their army. Almost every week boats arrive from Portugal to unload soldiers and war material.

About 350 African patriots are in PIDE prisons, and several hundred have been deported to the concentration camp on the island of Galinhas; in Bissao they are beginning to say that the postal service will soon stop working, since a large proportion of the employees are either in prison or have fled to neighbouring countries. The same applies to the National Overseas Bank, for the economic crisis has, and can have, no solution. In Cabo Verde, where misery reaches the limits of despair, particularly in the less favoured islands, more than a hundred young people have been arrested in Mindêlo and Praia and deported to the concentration camp of Tarrafal. Repressive security measures have been decreed against intellectuals enjoying great popularity.

But our struggle has won a victory of even greater importance, in the unity of Guinean and Cabo Verdian patriots resident in Guinea, within the PAIGC and the front which the PAIGC has created. The Portuguese colonialists, who have always tried to separate the Guineans from the Cabo Verdians, have been thrown into confusion by the solid unity of all the Africans. Today the prisons are full of Guineans and Cabo Verdians, and the struggle for the complete elimination of Portuguese colonialism has strengthened the ties of history and of blood which unite our two peoples.

Whatever the forces of the enemy, our victory over Portuguese colonialism depends mainly on ourselves, on our own militants. We must be conscious of the real forces at our disposal and base our revolutionary work on the popular masses.

However, it is obvious that the concrete aid and support of our neighbouring countries can play an important and decisive role if their leaders so wish. We are sure of the solidarity of all the African peoples in our struggle. We are conscious of the fact that our struggle for national liberation does not only serve our own peoples: it also serves the fundamental interests and the progress of all the peoples of Africa and of the world.

At the United Nations

*Extracts from a statement made in Conakry in
June 1962 to the United Nations Special Committee on
Territories under Portuguese Administration*

After the resolution on decolonialisation—the 1961 'reforms'

An analysis has been made of the position of the people of
Guinea as regards their relations with the metropolitan
country, the basic laws governing their lives, the
administrative structure and organisation, the political
institutions and how they function, the right to vote and its
exercise the organisation and administration of justice,
human rights and fundamental freedoms. That analysis
presents actual facts culled from legislation in force and
day-to-day reality.

The analysis makes clear that the constitutional, political,
legal, administrative and judicial status of Guinea, far from
that of being a 'province of Portugal' is that of a non-self-
governing country, conquered and occupied by force of
arms, ruled and administered by a foreign power. The
economic, political and social life of the people of Guinea
is governed by laws and rules which differ from those
applied to the people of Portugal; the people of Guinea have
no political rights, they do not help to operate the country's
institutions or to draft its laws, which, however, they must
obey; they do not elect representatives and cannot invest
political and administrative leaders with office or remove
them from office; they do not enjoy the most rudimentary
human rights or fundamental freedoms. Thus, far from
having their own legal identity, the people of Guinea are
a colonised and dependent people, whose dignity has been
deeply wounded. Neither directly nor indirectly do they
decide their present or future fate. Consequently there can
be no doubt that the people of Guinea are being deprived
of their right to self-determination, a right proclaimed and
established for all peoples in the United Nations Charter.

Nevertheless those who are not familiar with the actual facts
as regards the present position of the people of Guinea might
ask whether the recent Portuguese 'reforms' of colonial
legislation promulgated in 1961 have not significantly
changed the constitutional and legal status of Guinea.

As is well known, these 'reforms' of Portuguese colonial
legislation were instituted shortly after the United Nations
General Assembly, at its fifteenth session, had adopted the
resolution on decolonisation (14 December 1960). Before

proceeding further, it is worth noting that the hasty promulgation of such 'reforms' after the United Nations adopted that historic and constructive resolution is in itself a striking indictment by Portugal of its own colonial system.

An analysis of the legal texts of these 'reforms' will demonstrate whether they actually did or could change the constitutional and legal status of Guinea to any significant degree. The following legislation was enacted:

a) Decree no. 43,730, which revised articles 489,511 and 516 of the Overseas Administrative Reform Act;
b) Decree no. 43,894, approving the regulation of the occupation and granting of land concessions in the colonies;
c) Decree no. 43,895, establishing provincial settlement boards in the colonies;
d) Decree no. 43,896, organising the cantons in the colonies;
e) Decree no. 43,897, recognising the usages and customs regulating relations in private law in the colonies;
f) Decree no. 43,893, repealing the Native Statute of May 1954.

(Except for the first, all these decrees are dated 6 September, 1961.) Thus the matters affected by the enactment of the reforms are: *administrative organisation, land occupation, colonisation, justice and political status.*

In actual fact, this legislation made no significant change in those matters, nor was the practice of the Portuguese rulers greatly changed, and from the constitutional and legal standpoint the subjection of the people of Guinea to Portuguese colonialism. For example,

a) although Decree no. 43,730 states in its preamble: "in accordance with our administrative tradition, both overseas and in the metropolitan country, the commune is the basic administrative unit...", it still leaves local administration in the hands of the Portuguese authorities for it provides that the *mairies,* the municipal commissions and the local communities shall be presided over by persons appointed by the territorial or provincial governments.

b) Decree no. 43,894 deals with public property and with land concessions granted to settlers, administrative bodies and Catholic missions, and defines measures and establishes organs for the granting of such concessions. All in all, the law opens up to Portuguese settlers in Guinea opportunities for the occupation of land which either never existed before or were very limited.

c) Decree no. 43,895, which explicitly states in its preamble "... We have always regarded these as prerequisites for the desired progress in the overseas provinces, as one of the bases for the permanent establishment of European Portugal in the African territories . . .", is nothing more than a legal instrument for establishing effective organs and means for stimulating and achieving the long-desired permanent settlement of increased numbers of Europeans in Guinea.

d) Although Decree no 43,986 lays the basis for the organisation of the *regedorias,* it maintains the old system of replacing traditional chiefs by persons appointed by the colonial authorities.

e) Decree no. 43,897, while it recognises local usages and customs regulating relations to provide law, provides in its article 2 that such recognition shall be limited by the moral principles and basic rules of the Portuguese legal system. The scope of these limitations continues to be defined by article 138 of the political Constitution as "morality, the dictates of humanity and the *free exercise of Portuguese sovereignty"*.

f) Decree no. 43,893, which repeals the Native Statute, is the only official text in all the new legislation which should imply a change, however academic, in the colony's constitutional and legal status. But in point of fact that is not the case. In the prefatory statement, the reasons for repealing the Statute are candidly stated. It is said that the Statute is being repealed "because this law was not always understood in a way which did justice to the motives and intentions underlying it . . ." and because its existence "provided an opportunity for our enemies to assert that the Portuguese people are subject to two political laws and are consequently divided into two classes with no communication between them . . ." Thus the lawmakers' purpose was not to alter the motives and intentions underlying the Statute, which they do not condemn—despite the fact that the Statute had the effect of placing the African in Guinea in the position of having no identity in law and of being an *indigena*. The purpose of the lawmakers as disclosed in the prefatory statement, was to deprive the enemies of Portuguese colonialism of an effective weapon in the struggle on behalf of the Africans of Guinea—Portuguese law itself. But they did not succeed, for the following reasons.

First, the people of Guinea had no hand in drafting the new law, which is the result of a unilateral act, contrary to their legitimate aspirations. Secondly, Portuguese citizenship, fictitious as it is, is imposed on the African of Guinea without his consent. Although the Statute clearly defined the requirements for citizenship, there was never "any rush by the natives to secure the identity card which would make them citizens", as noted by Teixeira da Mota, a European investigator and official deputy in Guinea. The Africans of Guinea, from the time of the resistance in the colonial wars of conquest to the freedom struggle of today, never fought to acquire Portuguese citizenship. Thirdly, the law repealing the Native Statute was not followed by other legislation which would, in practice, regulate the participation of the people of Guinea in the management of their own affairs. Finally, the daily life of the people of Guinea (their economic, political, social and cultural life), with the exception of a few superficial alterations, particularly in the titles of laws, *has changed not one iota*. For example, although the 'indigenous' identity cards were and still are being hastily replaced by 'provisional' identity cards, the *indigena* tax and its 10 percent surtax were replaced by the annual personal income tax and the surtax, which not only amount to the same, but are still subject to the legislation governing the old taxes.

Consequently it is fair to say that far from changing the constitutional status of Guinea, the 1961 'reforms' merely made the situation worse, at least in the following respects.

a) By increasing the number of communes, creating additional local concentration of power and organising the cantons—which are always headed by persons appointed by the Governor—not only was Portuguese rule strengthened, but it was made easier for the colonial authorities to keep an eye on the Africans of Guinea and to carry out repressive measures against individuals and groups.

b) By defining procedures and establishing organs for the application and granting of land concessions to nonindigenous parties, more opportunities were provided for usurping and effectively occupying land which had until then belonged to the African communities.

c) By setting up the Provincial Settlement Boards, contrary to the spirit of the law itself, the way is being opened to European colonisation in Guinea to the detriment of the interests of the overwhelming majority of the people and of all classes of Africans.

Moreover, the 1961 'reforms' are contrary to the spirit of the provisions of resolutions 1542 (XV) and 1514 (XV) of the United Nations General Assembly, because they effect no change in the Portuguese political Constitution which, having been revised in 1961 with the clear intention of evading the obligations arising from the principles of the Charter, continues to state that Guinea is "an integral part of the Portuguese nation". Their purpose is to perpetuate the fiction of the 'overseas provinces' and they therefore constitute a flagrant violation of the right of the people of Guinea to self-determination and independence, while at the same time an attempt is made to baffle the vigilance of the forces fighting for freedom, particularly those of the United Nations.

But the Portuguese colonial government has never succeeded and never will succeed in attaining the objectives of the 1961 'reforms'. Despite all subterfuges, they fail to conceal the actual realities of the constitutional and legal status of the people of Guinea. These very 'reforms' show that, now as before, this status continues to be determined by:

a) the Portuguese political Constitution;
b) the Overseas Organic Law;
c) the administrative and Legal Statute of Guinea.

Moreover the organs of Portuguese sovereignty—the Head of the Portuguese State, the Portuguese National Assembly, the Portuguese Government and the Portuguese courts— still have the final say in the economic, political and social life of the colony. The National Assembly, the Council and the Portuguese Minister for Overseas Territories still hold special legislative powers with respect to Guinea. These metropolitan organs enjoy the co-operation of the Portuguese Corporative Chamber, the Conference of Overseas Governors, the Economic Conference of Overseas Portugal and other technical bodies. The Governor and the Government Council, the former exercising executive and legislative powers and the latter acting in an advisory capacity, are still the colony's organs of government. There has been no change either in the system of appointing the Governor or in the composition and the manner of appointment and election of the members of the Government Council.

Today, as yesterday, the Portuguese in Guinea are imbued with the same spirit in which, from the Middle Ages until our times, they practised the slave trade; the spirit in which they engaged in their cruel wars of conquest and occupation, in which they built up and organised, down to the smallest detail, the colonial exploitation of the country's human and natural resources, and which at present motivates the prevalent economic, police and military repression and furnishes the threat of a new colonial war which hangs over the people of Guinea. It is that spirit, which is a historical development of the Middle Ages, which determines and shapes Portugal's colonial legislation and methods.

Internal peace and security—repression

The laws and the daily realities of economic, political, social and cultural life to which the people of Guinea are subjected reveal that the people are the target of one of the most violent and best-organised examples of oppression (national, social and cultural) and economic exploitation in the history of colonialism. This system of oppression and economic exploitation was introduced and built up in Guinea by force of arms. Its development and continued implementation could be achieved only by recourse to armed repression (by the army and the police) and by the systematic use of violence in all its forms against any attempt at insurrection made by the people of Guinea.

The 'internal peace and security' imposed by Portuguese colonial domination in Guinea is not, and never has been, anything other than the fruit of a victory achieved by systematic repression, supported by an administrative framework which has engineered down to the most trifling detail its action against the long-standing desire for liberation and the active hatred of the people of Guinea for foreign domination. This situation has obtained from the times of the conquest and colonial occupation right up to the active struggle for national liberation which that people is waging today.

In the course of colonial wars lasting over half a century (1870-1936), hardly a year went by, as Teixeira da Mota admits, without some kind of military operations. These operations "had sometimes to be repeated over and over again against the same populations". The period from 1936 to 1959, after the administrative machine had been put together and set in motion, was one of silent repression, of secret recourse to violence, of unsung victims, of disorganised, individual reaction, of assaults and crimes of all sorts taking place within the four walls of the administrative buildings. Since 1959, in the face of the great strides of the African peoples along the road to national independence and of the firm resolution of the people of Guinea to free themselves from the Portuguese colonial yoke, there has been a return to open and undisguised repression by the army and police, in the towns as in the countryside, in private homes as in the public services, in the massacre of the indigenous populations as in the murder of nationalist prisoners.

A detailed and concrete study of the practical realities of the life of the people of Guinea and of the practices of the Portuguese overlords reveals that despite all the precautionary and repressive measures taken by the Portuguese colonialists, they have never actually experienced a real 'era of internal peace and security' in Guinea. One of the most interesting features of the Portuguese colonial laws is that despite all attempts at disguise, they disclose not only the intentions and actions of the Portuguese masters, but also the methods and means they resort to in order to preserve law and order and maintain their presence in peace and security.

Although the structure and organisation of Portuguese colonial domination display both in theory and in practice—down to the most insignificant details—a high degree of efficiency in exploiting the African population, the basic strength of Portuguese colonialism lies not in legal provisions nor in any original features of its political organisation. The basic strength of Portuguese colonialism, whether or not assisted by favourable historical circumstances, lies, and has always lain, in *its moral and physical propensity for repressive practices,* based on an absolute refusal to regard the African as a human being.

The cannon and other firearms of the era of discovery and conquest, the *palmatória,* the whip, the pistol, the modern rifle, the machine gun, the mortar, bombs of all kinds, including napalm bombs, and torture are the instruments of that strength. The navigators and mariners of former days, the mercenaries, the Captains General, the soldiers of the 'pacification', the sepoys, the *chefes de posto,* the Administrators, the Governors, the modern colonial troops (army, navy and air force) and the political police are its agents.

This is not the place for a recital of the crimes of Portuguese colonialism, of which world opinion is now well aware. It will suffice to recall that from the time of the slave hunts until the massacres of today, the people of Guinea have been the constant victims of these crimes.

a) More than a million Africans were carried off by the slave traders from the Guinea region.

b) Ten of thousands of Africans in Guinea were killed in the colonial wars of conquest and of occupation.

c) Few adult Africans—the so-called natives—have escaped the *palmatória* or the whip.

d) On August 3rd 1959, fifty African workers who had gone on strike were massacred on the docks at Pijiguiti (Bissao).

e) A number of African nationalists, including Joao Rosa, accountant, Antonio Teixeira, mechanic, and Joao Araujo, farmer, died of the tortures to which they were subjected by the political police (PIDE), in whose prisons more than 1,000 African nationalists have been incarcerated since 1957.

f) Over 300 nationalists are still held in the prisons of the PIDE, including: Fernando Fortes, post office employee; Epifânio Amado, assistant pharmacist; Inacio Semêdo, farmer; Quintino Nozolini, official; Mamadu Turé, barman; Bernardo Pereira, clerk; Malan Nanque, farmer; Eduardo Pinto, mechanic; Domingos Furtado, clerk; Renato Furtado, clerk.

g) Recently, hundreds of nationalist Africans have been sent to the concentration camp of the island of Galinhas.

h) Dozens of Africans have been killed in the bush by Portuguese troops, who burn down any villages thought to be rebellious.

i) Hardly a day passes, in town or countryside, without the rattle of machine-guns, the thud of mortars or the roar of aircraft engaged in the unceasing hunt for nationalists.

At the present time, as a means of repressing the nationalist forces, attempting to stifle the struggle for national liberation by the people of Guinea, and perpetuating their own domination, the Portuguese colonialists have available:

Armed forces
4,000 European soldiers
2,500 African soldiers
5 jet aircraft (fighters)
2 bomber aircraft
2 armed *avisos* (dispatch boats)
modern equipment including tanks and napalm bombs

Security forces
comprising 300 African men (including sepoys) commanded by European officers and sergeants

Political police (PIDE)
10 European special agents, and about 1,000 European and African intelligence agents, commanded by an inspector

The European population
most of whom act as unpaid intelligence agents for the PIDE

The government authorities
these supply information and serve the army as well as carrying out civil policy, in addition to engaging in repression on their own account.

An air base in the Cabo Verde islands, an airfield at Bissao and several airstrips in the interior and in the islands of Guinea are used for purposes of repression by the air force. Since Guinea is eight hours' flying time from Lisbon, the Portuguese colonialists also rely on the possibility of rushing in emergency reinforcements from the home country if neccessary.

As the struggle for national liberation takes shape, the number of African soldiers is being progressively decreased and that of European soldiers increased. The African soldiers are recruited by the government authorities and sent under duress to military camps. The European soldiers form part of special overseas contingents, detached to Guinea. The security police are recruited from among the sepoys and former soldiers. The intelligence agents of the political police are recruited among Africans who agree to betray their own people in order to protect their own positions or to obtain employment or a means of livelihood. The European agents are exclusively professionals, seasoned men from Portugal. Some of them attended the Nazi schools of repression.

Future prospects for the country

Although living under the threat of another colonial war—whose probable methods and atrocities are tragically and graphically illustrated in the action currently being undertaken by Portuguese colonialist forces against the people of Angola—the people of Guinea are determined to bring about an improvement in the situation of their country. They are resolved to live up to their tradition of resistance to foreign domination by putting a speedy end to Portuguese colonialism and laying down in freedom the groundwork for the progressive development of their African homeland.

The desire to throw off the colonial yoke and rid itself of foreign domination has always been one of the deepest aspirations of the people of Guinea. Wounded in their human dignity, deprived of any legal personality, they have never let slip any opportunity to manifest their non-acceptance of, aversion for and resistance to the 'Portuguese presence' in Guinea. The Africans of Guinea have had recourse to every means at their disposal, from individual opposition to collective action, from refusal to pay taxes to mass emigration, in order to defend their dignity and give proof of their love of freedom and hatred of foreign rule. Suffice it to recall that during the last forty years more than 50,000 Africans have left Guinea in order to settle in neighbouring territories; and also that to this very day, some groups, such as the inhabitants of the island of Canhabaque and of the Oio region (in the interior of the country) have not entirely submitted to Portuguese domination. A glance at the Portuguese colonial laws will show that they have been inspired by anxiety, by the need to remain vigilant and to repress the resistance of the African population of Guinea.

The people of Guinea love peace and freedom and wish to put an end to the misery, the suffering, the state of ignorance and the trepidation in which they live. Being aware of their rights in their own country, the people of Guinea aspire to freedom and wish to achieve progress and happiness in peace. But the Portuguese state has always evinced the utmost contempt for the legitimate aspirations of the people of Guinea. Moreover it has always replied to such demonstrations by resorting to the severest repressive measures.

In addition, the constitutional, legal, political and administrative situation of Guinea—the laws and practices of Portuguese colonialism—have never given the people of that country an opportunity of fulfilling their aspirations, or of making even gradual headway along the path of freedom and progress, 'within the framework of the Portuguese administration'. Thus there has never been more than one way in which the people of Guinea could attempt to fulfil their aspirations towards liberty and progress, namely, *by a struggle for national liberation.* Despite the particularly difficult conditions confronting them, the people of Guinea, guided by enlightened leaders who at an early stage foresaw the decline and end of the colonial era, roused themselves and in 1953, with courage and enthusiasm, plunged into the struggle for national liberation.

It was the actual internal conditions, the realities of their daily life, which decided the people of Guinea to undertake the struggle for national liberation and for the speedy and total liquidation of Portuguese colonialism. But the struggles and victories of other African peoples against foreign rule and the progress made by mankind in the realms of freedom, human dignity, social justice and international law have played no small part in influencing and strengthening that decision. That is why the fight of Guinea for national liberation is part and parcel of the struggle of the African peoples for the total abolition of foreign rule in Africa—for the final and irrevocable abolition of the colonial system—which is one of the outstanding features of contemporary history.

Starting in 1953, Africans of Guinea attempted to organise themselves in order to take up, in an orderly manner and by collective action, the defence of their rights and interests (economic, political, moral and cultural) against the injustice, discrimination and despotism of the Portuguese administration. Although they were concerned with the situation of the so-called 'indigenous' masses with which they had close links (principally in the urban areas), they were forced to confine these attempts at organisation, at least in appearance, to those Africans who at the time were called *asimilados* or *civilizados.* These attempts coincided with the return to Guinea of some Africans who, abroad and for the most part in Europe, had closely followed the evolution of colonial policy and the international situation after the Second World War. In Portugal, they had taken their first steps along the path of 're-Africanisation' and development of national consciousness together with African students from other Portuguese colonies.

All these attempts failed in the face of opposition from the administrative authorities, who went so far as to forbid the establishment of a sports and recreational association for Africans. Sensing that something new was occurring that affected the 'tranquillity' of the population, especially in Bissao, the authorities decided to keep close watch on suspect Africans. However, the vanguard of this nationalist movement (composed primarily of Guinean and Cabo Verdian civil servants and business employees) began secretly to mobilise the workers of Bissao into an organisation called the Movement for the National Independence of Guinea (MING).

In 1956, all attempts at lawful action having failed and because of the weakness of the MING, this same group of Africans, together with several craftsmen and manual workers, decided to create a clandestine organisation of the political party type to carry on the struggle for national liberation. Thus was born, in September of that year, the *Partido Africano da Independencia da Guiné e Cabo Verde* (PAIGC), the central organisation of the peoples of those colonies in the struggle for national liberation.

The PAIGC defined its fundamental objectives as follows (article 4 of the Statutes).

a) Immediate conquest of national independence in Guinea and the Cabo Verde Islands.

b) Democratization and emancipation of the African populations of these countries, exploited for centuries by Portuguese colonialism.

c) Achievement of rapid economic progress and true social and cultural advancement for the peoples of Guinea and the Cabo Verde Islands.

To win national independence, the PAIGC set itself the task of mobilising, organising and directing the Guinean and Cabo Verde masses in the struggle for the total abolition of Portuguese colonial rule (article 5 of the Statutes). Having proclaimed, in its manifesto, its intention to create the means necessary to "build peace, happiness and progress" in Guinea and the Cabo Verde Islands, the PAIGC defined a minor programme of "unity and struggle" and drew up a major programme* along the following general lines: immediate and total independence; national unification of Guinea and the Cabo Verde Islands; African unification; a democratic and anti-colonialist regime; economic independence, building up the economy and developing production; justice and progress for all; strong national defence with the participation of the people; an independent international policy, in the interests of the nation, Africa, peace and progress of mankind.

With regard to international policy, the PAIGC declared itself for "peaceful co-operation with all the peoples of the world" and expressed its acceptance of and respect for the principles of the United Nations Charter and those of the Bandung Conference.

Starting in 1958, after overcoming not only the difficulties of building up a clandestine military organisation while

* the complete text of this Party programme is given in the appendix

exposed to the dangers of Portuguese repression, by then reinforced (since 1957) by the active presence of the political police, but also the resistance to be expected in a society in which political organisations had always been forbidden, the PAIGC undertook to broaden the struggle for liberation both in Guinea and in the Cabo Verde Islands, limiting itself primarily, however, to the working masses and employees in the urban areas. This development was greatly accelerated after 1958, following the national independence of the Republic of Guinea, which opened up new prospects for the historical evolution of the African peoples.

The strikes of July-August 1959, suppressed by the massacre at the Pijiguiti dock, showed that the course followed until then had been a mistaken one. The urban centres proved to be the stronghold of colonialism, and mass demonstrations and representations were found to be not only ineffectual but also an easy target for the repressive and destructive operations of the colonialist forces.

Meeting clandestinely in Bissao in September 1959, the PAIGC adopted the following plan.

a) To reinforce the organisation in the urban areas, but to maintain it clandestinely and avoid all public demonstrations.

b) Urgently to mobilise and organise the rural masses, shown by experience to be the principal force in the struggle for national liberation.

c) To induce Africans of all ethnic groups, of all origins and of all social strata to unite around the Party.

d) To train the greatest possible number of persons, both at home and abroad, for the political leadership, the organisation and the development of the struggle.

e) To strengthen co-operation with the nationalist organisations of other Portuguese colonies, with the African countries, in particular the independent countries, and, further, with the democratic and progressive forces of the world, including those of Portugal. To develop effective action at the international level.

f) To organise or encourage the organisation of nationalist movements abroad, in particular among the émigrés residing in territories neighbouring on Guinea and the Cabo Verde Islands, to work for liberation and for the future of their people.

g) To increasingly strengthen and broaden the organisation, to train cadres in increasing numbers and to endeavour to obtain the necessary means for successfully pursuing the struggle. To expect the best, but to be prepared for the worst.

h) To train technical personnel at all levels, and, as far as possible, to study and plan the groundwork for and means of promoting rapid economic progress in Guinea and the Cabo Verde Islands.

In order to ensure the safety of some of its leaders and to develop the struggle abroad, the Party decided to transfer its general secretariat to Conakry. It was able to do so thanks to the fraternal support of the *Parti Démocratique* of the Republic of Guinea.

Although the colonialist forces soon launched the campaign of repression to which the country is still subjected (the first arrests of nationalists by the PIDE took place in April 1960), and although the colonial army and its equipment were greatly strengthened, within a little over two years the PAIGC succeeded in carrying out its plan and thus ensuring the successful continuation of the struggle it is directing. Thus

a) The Party organisation in the urban areas is today stronger than ever and remains clandestine, in the interests of the struggle, which has just entered a more active phase. This was recently proved most strikingly, at the time of the arrest of the Party's Chairman, Rafael Barbosa, who for eighteen months lived in hiding in Bissao. The organisation and discipline of the Party were such that it was able to contain the rebellious masses, and thus avoid the massacres which the colonialist forces expected to perpetrate.*

b) The peasant masses are, in the main, mobilised and organised throughout the country. Today, together with the workers and employees of the urban areas, they constitute the principal strength of the Party, to which they have given many of its best leaders.

c) Inside the country, all ethnic groups, all social strata, Africans of all origins, men and women, the young and the old, are solidly united around the Party. This is borne out by the non-existence in the country of any other organisation, by the fact that the people as a whole carry out the Party's instructions, and even by the presence within its leadership of nationalists from all social strata, all beliefs and most of the ethnic groups, men as well as women.

d) Hundreds of cadres (in politics, the trade union movement and the intensification of the struggle), most of them young people, have received their training from the Party and are now in the forefront of the continual mobilisation, organisation and education of the masses of the people, for the achievement of national independence,

*Rafael Barbosa was released by the Portuguese authorities in August 1969, after nearly eight years of imprisonment without trial. Ed.

its consolidation, and the political, economic, social and cultural building up of the country.

e) Co-operation with other nationalist organisations in the Portuguese colonies has been strengthened and organised. After the dissolution of the African Revolutionary Front for the National Independence of the Portuguese Colonies (FRAIN) set up in Tunis in January 1960 by the People's Movement for the Liberation of Angola (MPLA) and the PAIGC, these same organisations, together with those of Mozambique, Sao Tomé and Goa, created the Conference of Nationalist Organisations of the Portuguese Colonies (CONCP) at Casablanca in April 1961, with general secretariat headquarters at Rabat. The role of the CONCP is fundamentally that of co-ordinating the struggle of the peoples of the Portuguese colonies and ensuring unity, solidarity and co-operation.

At the African and Afro-Asian level, the PAIGC has now developed fruitful relations with the governments and parties of the independent countries and with the nationalist organisations of the countries as yet dependent. As an active member of the Conference of African Peoples and the Council of Solidarity of Afro-Asian Peoples, the PAIGC has participated in all international meetings concerned with the liberation of the colonial peoples. Similarly, it has visited several countries and secured the natural support of African countries (in particular the Republics of Guinea, Ghana, Senegal and Mali, and the Kingdom of Morocco), as well as the active solidarity of Asian countries.

At the international level, after the Secretary-General of the Party had revealed the crimes of Portuguese colonialism to world opinion, something done for the first time by an African from the Portuguese colonies, intensified and persistent action was taken to make known the true situation of the peoples under Portuguese domination and to obtain support and aid for their liberation. Thus the PAIGC enlisted not only the sympathy but also the active support, political in the main, of peace and freedom-loving peoples and governments, and also of democratic and progressive organisations, in the fight waged by the peoples of Guinea and the Cabo Verde Islands.

At the United Nations, the PAIGC has always expressed the legitimate aspirations of its people to national liberation and independence, and its confidence in the Organisation. Clearly emphasising the desire for peace and liberty which motivates its action, the PAIGC sent to the United Nations, among other documents, a memorandum addressed to the sixteenth session of the General Assembly, dated 26 September 1961, in which it proposed specific measures for the peaceful abolition of Portuguese rule.

Moreover, on the principle that the struggle it is directing is neither aimed against the Portuguese people nor contrary to their true interests, the PAIGC has established and developed contacts with Portuguese democratic elements, not only for the purpose of organically strengthening the struggle against Portugal's colonial-fascist regime, but also with a view to preserving the possibility of co-operation between the people of Guinea and the Cabo Verde Islands and the Portuguese people, on the basis of independence and of reciprocity of rights and duties.

f) Following suggestions and proposals made by the PAIGC either from within its home country or locally, the émigrés from Guinea and the Cabo Verde Islands residing in the neighbouring countries have created liberation 'movements.' In the Republic of Guinea, the Movement for the Liberation of Guinea and the Cabo Verde Islands (MLGCV, Conakry), organised with the help of the general secretariat of the PAIGC, groups all émigrés truly interested in the liberation of their people and works in close co-operation with that secretariat.

In July 1961, following an appeal for unity launched by the PAIGC in April 1961, the Conference of Nationalist Organisations of Guinea and the Cabo Verde Islands was held in Dakar. It was presided over by a leader of the Party, and several official bodies were represented. Following a proposal by the PAIGC, the Conference, by means of several resolutions, among them one creating the United Liberation Front of Guinea and the Cabo Verde Islands (FUL) which comprises the Party (the organisation inside the country) and the movements abroad (in the Republics of Guinea and Senegal), assumed the task of co-ordinating joint action in the struggle against Portuguese colonialism (articles I and II of the charter of the FUL).

The 'movements' in Senegal, paralysed by parochialism and by internal and inter-party conflicts and contradictions, were unable to consolidate their organisations (which broke up into a number of sub-groups), and failed to respect the commitments made at the Dakar Conference concerning the creation of the FUL, which they disavowed. These 'movements' have been unable thus far to co-operate usefully in the liberation struggle in which they propose to take part and, in addition, some of them have made difficulties for that struggle, principally by assuming negative attitudes and even attitudes contrary to the interests of the Republic of Senegal itself (we may cite as an example the attacks directed from that country's territory in July 1961, which were halted in time by the Senegalese Government).

At the present time, the PAIGC, which has the support of a large number of the émigrés from Guinea and the Cabo

Verde Islands living in Senegal, is sparing no efforts to ensure that, as in the Republic of Guinea, the émigrés who are really interested in the liberation of their people co-operate to the best effect with those carrying on the fight inside the country. In this endeavour has the fraternal sympathy of the Senegalese people and their Government.

Continually strengthening and expanding its organisation, the Party now covers all parts of the country. Its membership is constantly growing, particularly among the popular masses who are definitively committed to the struggle. Furthermore, the Party has never spared any effort to secure the ways and means for carrying on the fight to victory in the face of the Portuguese administration's systematic disregard for the aspirations of the people of Guinea. In pursuing those efforts, it has acted on the principle that liberation should be the work of the people themselves, who should rely primarily on their own resources to attain this goal.

Seeking a peaceful solution of its conflict with the Portuguese colonialists, the PAIGC took specific steps to try to persuade the Portuguese government to recognise the right of the people of Guinea and the Cabo Verde Islands to self-determination and national independence and by so doing to enhance the possibilities of co-operation between them and the Portuguese people. These steps which at the same time promoted the interests of international peace and security, included the dispatch of a 'memorandum' and an 'open letter' to the Portuguese government, dated 1 December 1960 and 13 October 1961 respectively. In this way specific proposals were submitted to the Portuguese government for the peaceful elimination of colonial rule in Guinea and the Cabo Verde Islands.

But the Portuguese government ignored these efforts, its only response being to reinforce its colonial troops and intensify its repression.

Confronted with the reactionary attitude of that Government and in particular its blatant contempt for the principles of the United Nations Charter and the resolutions adopted by the General Assembly at its fifteenth session, the PAIGC, acting in accordance with the will of the people of Guinea and recognising the urgent need to give practical aid to the people of Angola as a new colonial war of genocide was unleashed against them, proclaimed on 3 August 1961, the anniversary of the massacre of Pijiguiti quay, that the fight for liberation had passed from the purely political phase to the phase of direct action.

In accordance with the specific conditions of that fight and the plans for its development, direct action was limited to sabotage of the bases of colonial exploitation in Guinea. That decision was and continues to be applied in all parts of Guinea, and the action taken has proved to be an effective means of disrupting and disorganising colonialist exploitation.

Interpreting the peaceful attitude of the people of Guinea, the PAIGC still is and always has been desirous of reaching a peaceful solution of the conflict between them and the government of Portugal. Such a solution must not, however, be long in coming, for the people of Guinea, revolted by the crimes and outrages of Portuguese colonialist practice, mobilised, organised and prepared for the task of shaking off the colonial yoke, are willing to make any sacrifice to put an end to foreign rule. What is more, they are now capable of doing so.

If the United Nations itself and all the forces which are really in a position to influence the Portuguese government, with a view to making it respect international legality, prove unable to persuade that government to abandon its reactionary and criminal position, nothing will be able to stop the people of Guinea from resorting to all available means of eliminating once and for all the bases and agents of Portuguese rule. In such an event, the Portuguese government itself would obviously bear sole responsibility for whatever happened in Guinea.

In order to further the important task of consolidating independence and ensuring progress, the PAIGC is organising an extensive programme for the training of cadres (administration, production, health, tourism, etc.) and is putting it into effect as far as circumstances permit. It is eager to avail itself of every possible opportunity of proceeding as rapidly as possible with the training of a large body of personnel, particularly at the intermediate level, so that there will be African civil servants ready to go into action immediately following liberation.

These, then, if only in broad outline, are some of the specific aspects of the development of the fight for national liberation being waged by the people of Guinea. As far as the actual conduct of the struggle is concerned, its development, both within the country and abroad, has been determined fundamentally by the activities of the Party, which has its headquarters and the great majority of its active members and leaders inside the country.

Accordingly, it may be stated that national liberation offers the only prospect for Guinea's development. In other words, the necessary and indispensable condition for its development, in terms both of what the Guineans want and of cold fact, is today *national liberation*.

Although it is still in full process of development, the fight for liberation of the people of Guinea has already had certain positive results which, having strengthened it considerably, may be regarded as victories.

For example, it has increased the political awareness of the African masses, who had never before been permitted to exercise those essential functions of man—political thought and action.

It has intensified the feeling of unity of all Africans without distinction and is continuing to do so to an ever greater extent each day. In this connection, two facts are especially noteworthy. Firstly, the fight has erased the differences—many of which are carefully cultivated by the colonialists—between certain ethnic groups in Guinea, which are now united in the pursuit of national liberation and progress. Secondly, it has destroyed an important weapon on which the Portuguese colonialists were relying in their effort to 'resist' the overwhelming desire of the people of Guinea for freedom: the conflict, often superficial and always based on material considerations, between the Cabo Verde minority, deliberately favoured by the colonialists in the matter of public service employment, and the *asimilados* among the native majority. Today, the people of Guinea and the people of Cabo Verde, whether behind prison walls or in hiding in the bush, are increasingly strengthening their unity, sharing a common ideal and acting together for the cause of national liberation and progress.

It has developed and is increasingly strengthening the national consciousness of a free and just fatherland for which all ethnic groups, all religious communities, all men and women are fighting.

Gradually overcoming the complexes engendered by colonial exploitation, it has enabled the 'marginal' human beings who are the product of colonialism to recover their personality as Africans. It has reawakened among the Africans of Guinea in general a feeling of confidence in the future.

It has made the personality of Guinea as an African nation known to the rest of the world, has given its people prestige and has won them the sympathy and friendship of other peoples.

It has influenced and is continuing strongly to influence the development of the fight for liberation in the Cabo Verde Islands, whose people are indissolubly linked with those of Guinea by ties of history and of blood.

It has encouraged the fight for liberation of the peoples of the other Portuguese colonies, has materially assisted the people of Angola in their struggle by making it necessary for the Portuguese colonialists to divert some of their troops from that country, and in general has served the cause of Africa's liberation from foreign rule.

In addition to these results, however, the fight of the people of Guinea has begun to have a significant effect on the actions of the Portuguese colonialists themselves. For example it has helped to bring about a gradual deterioration in the economy of Portugal as a nation oppressing other nations, for in carrying out its repressive policies Portugal is obliged to spend more and more money and is meeting with increasingly stubborn resistance from those nations.

It has shaken the morale and upset the material life of the families of the colonialists, who have had to send most of the European women and children back to Portugal with the consent of the authorities, because of growing insecurity.

It has obliged the colonial authorities to spend considerable amounts on bribing certain Africans and has caused them to lose confidence in the indigenous troops, in whom they formerly had great trust, and even in some of their own collaborators.

It has obliged the Portuguese state for the first time in history to nominate certain Africans to posts of responsibility, including that of deputy in Guinea.

It has helped to bring about a decline in the income of colonialist commercial and financial enterprises and to aggravate considerably the colony's unfavourable balance of trade during the past three years, thereby worsening Portugal's economic situation.

It has provoked and deepened differences of opinion among Europeans living in Guinea, particularly in the Portuguese army, from whose ranks there have been a considerable number of desertions.

It has obliged the administrative authorities to abandon certain repressive measures, such as those applied in connection with the collection of taxes, and has been one of the causes, together with the United Nations resolution on decolonisation, of the promulgation of the 'reforms' of 1961 and the repeal, if only in theory, of the *Estatuto dos Indígenas*.

Accession to independence

The people of Guinea are fighting for their right to self-determination and national independence. They wish to decide their future for themselves, free from any kind of foreign intervention in affairs which are their exclusive concern. They wish to shake off the colonial yoke completely so that they may form a free and sovereign nation in a new and independent Africa.

The people of Guinea know very well that the procedures and methods to be adopted for the prompt restoration of their right to self-determination, for the immediate elimination of Portuguese colonial rule and for the attainment of national independence do not depend on their wishes alone. If that were true, Guinea would already be an independent country and accordingly the situation of its people would not be an international problem.

The people of Guinea consider that the re-establishment of international legality in their country—with respect for the right to self-determination, the elimination of colonialism and the attainment of national independence—depend essentially on the following factors:

a) their own desire and determination to free themselves from the colonial yoke, as manifested in the means and the human and material resources which are available to them for the attainment of this goal;

b) the attitude and conduct (moral, political and legal) of the Portuguese government as a party directly concerned in the matter;

c) international politics, that is, the result of internal and external factors which determine at the international level the specific action (positive or negative) both of governments (considered individually or as members of international assemblies) and of the United Nations itself;

d) the time required for the contradictions inherent in each of the above factors, which are constantly in a state of flux, to be defined, to develop and to straighten themselves out, whether by peaceful or non-peaceful means.

Where the United Nations is concerned, the problem of this people's national independence may be summarised in the following two alternatives: (1) either the United Nations, duly supported by the democratic forces of the world, will succeed in planning and putting into effect practical measures compelling the Portuguese government to respect the Charter and the resolution on decolonialisation, to abide by international legality, to renounce a position which is contrary to civilised interests and to desist from a crime against humanity, or (2) the United Nations, through lack of support, methods and practical measures, or some or all of these factors, will not succeed in persuading the Portuguese government to abandon its stubborn and absurd attitude.

In the former case—which may be called 'effective recognition by the Portuguese government of the respect it owes to the United Nations'—we would have the hypothesis of that government accepting the peaceful elimination of Portuguese colonial domination by negotiation. The attitude of the people of Guinea, as interpreted by its legitimate representatives, would obviously be the one already defined for such a hypothesis. Not only would the prestige of the United Nations be maintained (it would show that the resolution on decolonialisation can indeed be put into effect), but it would also be possible to take into account Portuguese interests in that country, while stubbornly defending the rights of the people of Guinea. Thus it would still be possible to provide for the possibility of studying and defining the participation and assistance of the United Nations in the practical solution of the problem at issue, through its representatives who are most versed in these matters.

In the second case, the hypothesis that peaceful means can be used to eliminate Portuguese colonialism in Guinea would cease to have any meaning, perhaps even less meaning than in the case of a refusal by the Portuguese government without United Nations intervention. The prestige of the United Nations would be seriously jeopardised, the resolution on decolonialisation would run the risk of being regarded as an academic exercise in international law and the people of Guinea would be obliged to use all means within their power to put an end to the crime perpetrated by the Portuguese government against itself and against mankind.

It is therefore justifiable to conclude that the United Nations' opportunity of contributing to the peaceful solution of the dispute between the people of Guinea and the Portuguese government does not depend on that people, which is seeking national independence and fighting for it, but on the nature and dynamic of the relations, whether peaceful or not, between that international Organisation and the Portuguese state. Hence, the measures which will have to be taken to secure the accession of the people of Guinea to national independence will also not depend—at least not immediately—on the people of Guinea, but above all on the United Nations, since that Organisation, as the guardian and trustee of international law, is the only body which can compel the Portuguese government to agree to the negotiations in which those measures would be defined.

The people of Guinea, reaffirming its confidence in the United Nations, hopes that the Organisation will not fail urgently to adopt specific and effective measures to oblige the Portuguese government to respect international law, and thus fulfil the weighty responsibilities incumbent upon it for the final elimination of colonialism in Guinea.

Anonymous soldiers for the United Nations

Extracts from a declaration to the Fourth Commission of the UN General Assembly, December 12, 1962

The UN resolution on decolonialisation has created a new situation for our struggle. Having been condemned, the *colonial system,* whose immediate and total elimination is demanded by this resolution, is now an international crime. We have thus obtained a legal basis for demanding the elimination of the colonial yoke in our country and for using all necessary means to destroy that yoke. But this applies not only to us. On the basis of the resolution, the United Nations and the anti-colonialist states and organisations—all the forces of peace in the world—can and must take concrete action against the Portuguese state. Illegally and against the interests of civilisation, the Portuguese state is continuing to perpetrate both in our country and in other African countries the 'crime of colonialisation', thus endangering international peace and security.

We are certain that the Portuguese government cannot persist with impunity in committing an international crime. We are also certain that the United Nations has at its disposal all the means necessary to conceive and carry out concrete and effective measures both to make the principles of the Charter be respected and to impose international legality in our countries and to defend the interests of peace and of civilisation.

We are not here to ask the UN to send troops to free our countries from the Portuguese colonial yoke. Perhaps we could ask for it, but we do not think it necessary, for we are confident that we will be able to free our countries. We invoke only one right: the right to obtain collaboration and concrete assistance from the UN in order to hasten the liberation of our countries from the colonial yoke and thus to lessen the human and material losses which a long struggle can cause.

Our struggle has lost its strictly national character and has moved onto an international level. The struggle taking place in our country today is the struggle of progress against misery and suffering, of freedom against oppression. While it is true that the victims of this struggle are none other than the children of our people, it is nevertheless true that each of our comrades who dies under torture or falls under the fire of the Portuguese colonialist machine-guns identifies himself, through the hopes and certainties which we all carry in our hearts and minds, with all men who love peace and freedom and wish to live a life of progress and happiness.

We are not just fighting for the realisation of our aspirations to freedom and national independence. We are fighting—and will fight until final victory—so that the resolutions and the Charter of the United Nations will be respected. In the prisons, in the towns and in the countryside of our land the battle is being fought today between the UN, which demands the elimination of the colonial system of domination of peoples, and the armed forces of the Portuguese government, which wishes to perpetuate this system against the legitimate rights of our people.

Who are we in fact, waging this struggle against the Portuguese colonialists in particularly difficult conditions?

When in Elizabethville or in the Congo bush a soldier of Indian, Ethiopian or other nationality falls under the fire of the enemy, he is one more victim who has given his life for the cause of the UN. He dies for a just ideal, since he believes that the UN resolutions on the Congo were aimed at achieving unity, peace and progress for the Congolese people in the independence which they reconquered and to which they have a right.

To have its resolutions respected, the UN has mobilised soldiers, pilots, administrators, technicians and experts of all sorts, and is spending enormous sums each day.

When in our country a comrade dies under police torture, is assassinated in prison, is burned alive or falls under the bullets of Portuguese guns, for which cause is he giving his life?

He is giving it for the liberation of our people from the colonial yoke, and hence for the UN. In fighting and dying for the liberation of our countries we are giving our lives, in the present context of international legality, for the ideal which the UN itself has defined in its Charter, in its resolutions, and in particular in its resolution on decolonialisation.

For us, the only difference between the Indian soldier, the Italian pilot or the Swedish administrator who dies in the Congo and our comrade who dies in Guinea or the Cabo Verde Islands is that by acting in our country for the same ideal we are simply *anonymous soldiers for the UN*.

The names of our comrades who have fallen victims of the Portuguese colonialists are not on the files of the UN. We have never been paid or equipped by the UN, nor do we have any budget assigned to cover the ever-increasing costs of our struggle. But in the uneven struggle which we are forced to wage we are nonetheless at the service of the UN, defending its prestige and the respect owed by all governments to the resolutions of an international character which it has adopted.

National liberation and peace, cornerstones of non-alignment

Extracts from a speech made in Cairo to the
2nd Conference of Heads of State and Governments
of Non-Aligned Countries, 1964

For some days we have been following with great attention the speeches in the general debate. For us these speeches have given us grounds to feel proud and have greatly encouraged us in our liberating struggle.

In your speeches, you have unanimously condemned imperialism and every sort of foreign domination as being the main source of the tensions, the suffering and the dangers which burden humanity. You have unequivocally reaffirmed your hatred of war, of foreign military bases and of recourse to violence as a means of settling conflicts between ideologies, between nations and between states. You have fiercely defended peaceful co-existence, loyal and constructive international co-operation and the need for equitable sharing of the world's riches, which have been created by man. By an argument as intelligent as it is free from prejudice you have shown that the banning of nuclear tests and weapons, as well as general and total disarmament, have become a necessary condition for guaranteeing the survival of the human species and even of our planet. In your just and exemplary aspiration to serve humanity you have reaffirmed your support for the principles of the United Nations Charter. You have thus shown your firm determination to work effectively for the immediate liberation of that Organisation, which is at present a giant with its hands tied, so that, its structure renewed, its institutions democratised and its voice strengthened to include those of hundreds of millions of human beings, it may fully serve the noble causes of freedom, fraternity, progress and happiness for mankind.

But you have done more than this. Faithfully translating the unanimous feelings of active solidarity of your peoples with our liberation struggle, you have given a striking proof of your position as combatants for liberty. You, our fellow combatants, at present occupy the place of honour which history has reserved for you and which allows you to contribute by all necessary means to the pressing elimination of colonial domination in our countries.

In the framework of your concrete solidarity with the national liberation of peoples and with their inalienable right to control their own destinies—one of the cornerstones of non-alignment—you have also, directly or indirectly, given your fraternal support to the peoples of heroic and socialist Cuba, of South Vietnam, indefatigable and victorious combatants, of Cyprus and of the Congo, tragically related by the blow of brazen foreign intervention, of martyrised Arab Palestine and of Puerto Rico, that small island which is so often forgotten and in which, as the evidence of its delegation has shown us, more than two million human beings are still suffering under the double yoke of imperialism and colonialism and are struggling, despite the power which faces them, for national independence.

Mr President, Your Majesties, Your Exellencies, the walls of the University of Cairo will guard with understandable zeal the echoes of your speeches, which have been so many commitments and lessons of humanism. And tomorrow, in the course of research into notable contributions to the well-being of humanity, people may well ask themselves whether, given the limitations imposed on the United Nations in this year 1964, the Conference of Non-Aligned Countries, in which no spectre can stifle the freedom to be *free* or fidelity to principles, has not constituted the most important or at least the most effective international organisation of our times.

Mr President, before returning to continue the political and armed struggle for the liberation of our peoples, we wish to reaffirm our active confidence in the practical value of this high international gathering. For our part, we are aware that the complex nature of our struggle is not limited simply to the elimination of the colonial yoke. Whether we wish it or not, we are fighting against imperialism, which is the basis of colonialism, in every form.

It is on the basis of this universal principle that we would like to express our firm conviction that our struggle, be it purely political or armed, is also an expression of the great struggle for peaceful co-existence and for peace. We want to carry out, at least, a policy of peaceful co-existence and peace with all peoples and all states, but in our concrete situation we consider that our very existence as free and independent nations and states is a sine qua non for this policy of co-existence and peace. To co-exist one must first of all exist, so the imperialists and the colonialists must be forced to retreat so that we can make a new contribution to human civilisation, based on the work, the dynamic personality and the culture of our peoples.

To make this contribution in independence, fraternity and equality with all peoples, it does not seem to us to be necessary to get involved in the ideological disputes and conflicts which are splitting the world. We do not need to follow any line: our position must be and remain based on the fundamental aspirations of our peoples. There is, however, in our ethic of non-alignment one vital need for alignment: we must be capable—and free—to adopt without equivocation any position which aims to serve the dignity, emancipation and progress of peoples.

Mr President, Your Majesties, Your Excellencies, you all represent peoples who have had experience in the struggle for national liberation, albeit to differing degrees, according to the diversity of your historical conditions. Thus you know better than we do that this struggle is in its very essence a daily capitalisation of efforts and sacrifices for a better life and for social liberation. Allow us to affirm to you that the policy of non-alignment which was defined three years ago in Belgrade and has been strengthened during this Conference, is a guarantee for the efforts and sacrifices capitalised by our peoples for their total liberation from every sort of oppression.

Brief Analysis of the Social Structure in Guinea

Condensed text of a seminar held in the Frantz Fanon Centre in Treviglio, Milan, from May 1 to 3, 1964

I should like to tell you something about the situation in our country, 'Portuguese' Guinea, beginning with an analysis of the social situation, which has served as the basis for our struggle for national liberation. I shall make a distinction between the rural areas and the towns, or rather the urban centres, not that these are to be considered mutually opposed.

In the rural areas we have found it necessary to distinguish between two distinct groups: on the one hand, the group which we consider semi-feudal, represented by the Fulas, and, on the other hand, the group which we consider, so to speak, without any defined form of state organisation, represented by the Balantes. There are a number of intermediary positions between these two extreme ethnic groups (as regards the social situation). I should like to point out straight away that although in general the semi-feudal groups were Muslim and the groups without any form of state organisations were animist, there was one ethnic group among the animists, the Mandjacks, which had forms of social relations which could be considered feudal at the time when the Portuguese came to Guinea.

I should now like to give you a quick idea of the social stratification among the Fulas. We consider that the chiefs, the nobles and the religious figures form one group; after them come the artisans and the Dyulas, who are itinerant traders, and then after that come the peasants properly speaking. I don't want to give a very thorough analysis of the economic situation of each of these groups now, but I would like to say that although certain traditions concerning collective ownership of the land have been preserved, the chiefs and their entourages have retained considerable privileges as regards ownership of land and the utilisation of other people's labour; this means that the peasants who depend on the chiefs are obliged to work for these chiefs for a certain period of each year. The artisans, whether blacksmiths (which is the lowest occupation) or leather-workers or whatever, play an extremely important role in the socio-economic life of the Fulas and represent what you might call the embryo of industry. The Dyulas, whom some people consider should be placed above the artisans, do not really have such importance among the Fulas; they are the people who have the potential—which they sometimes realise—of accumulating money. In general the peasants have no rights and they are the really exploited group in Fula society.

Apart from the question of ownership and property, there is another element which it is extremely interesting to compare and that is the position of women. Among the Fulas women have no rights; they take part in production but they do not own what they produce. Besides, polygamy is a highly respected institution and women are to a certain extent considered the property of their husbands.

Among the Balantes, which are at the opposite extreme, we find a society without any social stratification: there is just a council of elders in each village or group of villages who decide on the day to day problems. In the Balante group property and land are considered to belong to the village but each family receives the amount of land needed to ensure subsistence for itself, and the means of production, or rather the instruments of production, are not collective but are owned by families or individuals.

The position of women must also be mentioned when talking about the Balantes. The Balantes still retain certain tendencies towards polygamy, although it is mainly a monogamous society. Among the Balantes women participate in production but they own what they produce and this gives Balante women a position which we consider privileged, as they are fairly free; the only point on which they are not free is that children belong to the head of the family and the head of the family, the husband, always claims any children his wife may have: this is obviously to be explained by the actual economy of the group where a family's strength is ultimately represented by the number of hands there are to cultivate the land.

As I have said, there are a number of intermediate positions between these two extremes. In the rural areas I should mention the small African farm owners; this is a numerically small group but all the same it has a certain importance and has proved to be highly active in the national liberation struggle. In the towns (I shall not talk about the presence of Europeans in the rural areas as there are none in Guinea) we must first distinguish between the Europeans and the Africans. The Europeans can easily be classified as they retain in Guinea the social stratification of Portugal (obviously depending on the function they exercise in Guinea). In the first place, there are the high officials and the managers of enterprises who form a stratum with practically no contact with the other European strata. After that there are the medium officials, the small European traders, the people employed in commerce and the members of the liberal professions. After that come the workers, who are mainly skilled workers.

Among the Africans we find the higher officials, the middle officials and the members of the liberal professions forming a group; then come the petty officials, those employed in commerce with a contract, who are to be distinguished from those employed in commerce without a contract, who can be fired at any moment. The small farm owners also fall into this group; by assimilation we call all these members of the African petty bourgeoisie (obviously, if we were to make a more thorough analysis the higher African officials as well as the middle officials and the members of the liberal professions should also be included in the petty bourgeoisie). Next come the wage-earners (whom we define as those employed in commerce without any contract); among these there are certain important sub-groups such as the dockworkers, the people employed on the boats carrying goods and agricultural produce; there are also the domestic servants, who are mostly men in Guinea; there are the people working in repair shops and small factories and there are also the people who work in shops as porters and suchlike—these all come under the heading of wage-earners. You will notice that we are careful not to call these groups the proletariat or working class.

There is another group of people whom we call the *déclassés,* in which there are two sub-groups to be distinguished: the first sub-group is easy to identify—it is what would be called the lumpenproletariat if there was a real proletariat: it consists of really *déclassé* people, such as beggars, prostitutes and so on. The other group is not really made up of *déclassé* people, but we have not yet found the exact term for it; it is a group to which we have paid a lot of attention and it has proved to be extremely important in the national liberation struggle. It is mostly made up of young people who are connected to petty bourgeois or workers' families, who have recently arrived from the rural areas and generally do not work; they thus have close relations with the rural areas, as well as with the towns (and even with the Europeans). They sometimes live off one kind of work or another, but they generally live at the expense of their families. Here I should just like to point out a difference between Europe and Africa; in Africa there is a tradition which requires that, for example, if I have an uncle living in the town, I can come in and live in his house without working and he will feed me and house me. This creates a certain stratum of people who experience urban life and who can, as we shall see, play a very important role.

That is a very brief analysis of the general situation in Guinea, but you will understand that this analysis has no value unless it is related to the actual struggle. In outline, the methodological approach we have used has been as follows: first, the position of each group must be defined— to what extent and in what way does each group depend on the colonial regime? Next we have to see what position they adopt towards the national liberation struggle. Then we have to study their nationalist capacity and lastly, envisaging the post-independence period, their revolutionary capacity.

Among the Fulas the first group—the chiefs and their entourages—are tied to colonialism; this is particularly the case with the Fulas as in Guinea the Fulas were already conquerors (the Portuguese allied themselves with the Fulas in order to dominate Guinea at the beginning of the conquest). Thus the chiefs (and their authority as chiefs) are very closely tied to the Portuguese authorities. The artisans are extremely dependent on the chiefs; they live off what they make for the chiefs who are the only ones that can acquire their products, so there are some artisans who are simply content to follow the chiefs; then there are other people who try to break away and are well-disposed towards opposition to Portuguese colonialism. The main point about the Dyulas is that their permanent preoccupation is to protect their own personal interests; at least in Guinea, the Dyulas are not settled in any one place, they are itinerant traders without any real roots anywhere and their fundamental aim is to make bigger and bigger profits. It is precisely the fact that they are almost permanently on the move which provided us with a most valuable element in the struggle. It goes without saying that there are some who have not supported our struggle and there are some who have been used as agents against us by the Portuguese, but there are some whom we have been able to use to mobilise people, at least as far as spreading the initial ideas of the struggle was concerned—all we had to do was give them some reward, as they usually would not do anything without being paid.

Obviously, the group with the greatest interest in the struggle is the peasantry, given the nature of the various different societies in Guinea (feudal, semi-feudal, etc.) and the various degrees of exploitation to which they are subjected; but the question is not simply one of objective interest.

Given the general context of our traditions, or rather the superstructure created by the economic conditions in Guinea, the Fula peasants have a strong tendency to follow their chiefs. Thorough and intensive work was therefore needed to mobilise them. Among the Balantes and the groups without any defined form of state organisation the first point to note is that there are still a lot of remnants of animist traditions even among the Muslims in Guinea; the part of the population which follows Islam is not really Islamic but rather Islamised: they are animists who have adopted some Muslim practices, but are still thoroughly impregnated with animist conceptions. What is more, these groups without any defined organisation put up much more resistance against the Portuguese than the others and they have maintained intact their tradition of resistance to colonial penetration. This is the group that we found most ready to accept the idea of national liberation.

Here I should like to broach one key problem, which is of enormous importance for us, as we are a country of peasants, and that is the problem of whether or not the peasantry represents the main revolutionary force. I shall confine myself to my own country, Guinea, where it must be said at once that the peasantry is not a revolutionary force —which may seem strange, particularly as we have based the whole of our armed liberation struggle on the peasantry. A distinction must be drawn between a physical force and a revolutionary force; physically, the peasantry is a great force in Guinea: it is almost the whole of the population, it controls the nation's wealth, it is the peasantry which produces; but we know from experience what trouble we had convincing the peasantry to fight. This is a problem I shall come back to later; here I should just like to refer to what the previous speaker said about China. The conditions of the peasantry in China were very different: the peasantry had a history of revolt, but this was not the case in Guinea, and so it was not possible for our party militants and propaganda workers to find the same kind of welcome among the peasantry in Guinea for the idea of national liberation as the idea found in China. All the same, in certain parts of the country and among certain groups we found a very warm welcome, even right at the start. In other groups and in other areas all this had to be won.

Then there are the positions vis-à-vis the struggle of the various groups in the towns to be considered. The Europeans are, in general, hostile to the idea of national liberation; they are the human instruments of the colonial state in our country and they therefore reject a priori any idea of national liberation there. It has to be said that the Europeans most bitterly opposed to the idea of national liberation are the workers, while we have sometimes found considerable sympathy for our struggle among certain members of the European petty bourgeoisie.

As for the Africans, the petty bourgeoisie can be divided into three sub-groups as regards the national liberation struggle. First, there is the petty bourgeoisie which is heavily committed, and compromised with colonialism: this includes most of the higher officials and some members of the liberal professions. Second, there is the group which we perhaps incorrectly call the revolutionary petty bourgeoisie: this is the part of the petty bourgeoisie which is nationalist and which was the source of the idea of the national liberation struggle in Guinea. In between lies the part of the petty bourgeoisie which has never been able to make up its mind between the national liberation struggle and the Portuguese. Next come the wage-earners, which you can compare roughly with the proletariat in European societies, although they are not exactly the same thing: here, too, there is a majority committed to the struggle, but, again, many members of this group were not easy to mobilise—wage-earners who had an extremely petty bourgeois mentality and whose only aim was to defend the little they had already acquired.

Next come the *déclassés*. The really *déclassé* people, the permanent layabouts, the prostitutes and so on have been a great help to the Portuguese police in giving them information; this group has been outrightly against our struggle, perhaps unconsciously so, but nonetheless against our struggle. On the other hand, the particular group I mentioned earlier, for which we have not yet found any precise classification (the group of mainly young people recently arrived from the rural areas with contacts in both the urban and the rural areas) gradually comes to make a comparison between the standard of living of their own families and that of the Portuguese; they begin to understand the sacrifices being borne by the Africans. They have proved extremely dynamic in the struggle. Many of these people joined the struggle right from the beginning and it is among this group that we found many of the cadres whom we have since trained.

The importance of this urban experience lies in the fact that it allows comparison: this is the key stimulant required for the awakening of consciousness. It is interesting to note that Algerian nationalism largely sprang up among the émigré workers in France. As far as Guinea is concerned, the idea of the national liberation struggle was born not abroad but in our own country, in a milieu where people were subjected to close and incessant exploitation. Many people say that it is the peasants who carry the burden of exploitation: this may be true, but so far as the struggle is concerned it must be realised that it is not the degree of suffering and hardship involved as such that matters: even extreme suffering in itself does not necessarily produce the *prise de conscience* required for the national liberation struggle. In Guinea the peasants are subjected to a kind of exploitation equivalent to slavery; but even if you try and explain to them that they are being exploited and robbed, it is difficult to convince them by means of an unexperienced explanation of a technico-economic kind that they are the most exploited people; whereas it is easier to convince the workers and the people employed in the towns who earn, say, 10 escudos a day for a job in which a European earns between 30 and 50 that they are being subjected to massive exploitation and injustice, because they can see. To take my own case as a member of the petty bourgeois group which launched the struggle in Guinea, I was an agronomist working under a European who everybody knew was one of the biggest idiots in Guinea; I could have taught him his job with my eyes shut but he was the boss: this is something which counts a lot, this is the confrontation which really matters. This is of major importance when considering where the initial idea of the struggle came from.

Another major task was to examine the material interests and the aspirations of each group after the liberation, as well as their revolutionary capacities. As I have already said, we do not consider that the peasantry in Guinea has a revolutionary capacity. First of all we had to make an analysis of all these groups and of the contradictions between them and within them so as to be able to locate them all vis-à-vis the struggle and the revolution.

The first point is to decide what is the major contradiction at the moment when the struggle begins. For us the main contradiction was that between, on the one hand, the Portuguese and international bourgeoisie which was exploiting our people and on the other hand, the interests of our people. There are also major contradictions within the country itself, i.e. in the internal life of our country. It is our opinion that if we get rid of colonialism in Guinea the main contradiction remaining, the one which will then become the principal contradiction, is that between the ruling classes, the semi-feudal groups, and the members of the groups without any defined form of organisation. The first thing to note is that the conquest carried out first by the Mandingues and then by the Fulas was a struggle between two opposite poles which was blocked by the very strong structure of the animist groups. There are other contradictions, such as that between the various feudal groups and that between the upper group and the lower. All this is extremely important for the future, and even while the struggle is still going on we must begin to exploit the contradiction between the Fula people and their chiefs, who are very close to the Portuguese. There is a further contradiction, particularly among the animists, between the collective ownership of the land and the private ownership of the means of production in agriculture. I am not trying to stretch alien concepts here, this is an observation that can be made on the spot: the land belongs to the village, but what is produced belongs to whoever produces it—usually the family or the head of the family.

There are other contradictions which we consider secondary: you may be surprised to know that we consider the contradictions between the tribes a secondary one; we could discuss this at length, but we consider that there are many more contradictions between what you might call the economic tribes in the capitalist countries than there are between the ethnic tribes in Guinea. Our struggle for national liberation and the work done by our Party have shown that this contradiction is really not so important; the Portuguese counted on it a lot but as soon as we organised the liberation struggle properly the contradiction between the tribes proved to be a feeble, secondary contradiction. This does not mean that we do not need to pay attention to this contradiction; we reject both the positions which are to be found in Africa—one which says: there are no tribes, we are all the same, we are all one people in one terrible unity, our party comprises everybody; the other saying: tribes exist, we must base parties on tribes. Our position lies between the two, but at the same time we are fully conscious that this is a problem which must constantly be kept in mind; structural, organisational and other measures must be taken to ensure that this contradiction does not explode and become a more important contradiction.

As for contradictions between the urban and rural areas; I would say that there is no conflict between the towns and the countryside, not least because we are only town dwellers who have just moved from the country; everybody in the towns in Guinea has close relatives in the country and all town dwellers still engage in some peasant activity (growing crops etc.); all the same, there is a potential contradiction between the towns and the countryside which colonialism tries to aggravate.

That, in brief, is the analysis we have made of the situation; this has led us to the following conclusion: we must try to unite everybody in the national liberation struggle against the Portuguese colonialists: this is where our main contradiction lies, but it is also imperative to organise things so that we always have an instrument available which can solve all the other contradictions. This is what convinced us of the absolute necessity of creating a party during the national liberation struggle. There are some people who interpret our Party as a front; perhaps our Party is a front at the moment, but within the framework of the front there is our Party which is directing the front, and there are no other parties in the front. For the circumstances of the struggle we maintain a general aspect, but within the framework of the struggle we know what our Party is, we know where the Party finishes and where the people who just rallied for the liberation struggle begin.

When we had made our analysis, there were still many theoretical and practical problems left in front of us. We had some knowledge of other experiences and we knew that a struggle of the kind we hoped to lead—and win—had to be led by the working class; we looked for the working class in Guinea and did not find it. Other examples showed us that things were begun by some revolutionary intellectuals. What then were we to do? We were just group of petty bourgeois who were driven by the reality of life in Guinea, by the sufferings we had to endure, and also by the influence events in Africa and elsewhere had on us, in particular the experiences some of us acquired in Portugal and other countries in Europe, to try and do something.

And so this little group began. We first thought of a general movement of national liberation, but this immediately proved unfeasible. We decided to extend our activity to the workers in the towns, and we had some success with this; we launched moves for higher wages, better working conditions and so on. I do not want to go into details here, the only point I want to make is that we obviously did not have a proletariat. We quite clearly lacked revolutionary intellectuals, so we had to start searching, given that we—rightly—did not believe in the revolutionary capacity of the peasantry.

One important group in the towns were the dockworkers; another important group were the people working in the boats carrying merchandise, who mostly live in Bissao itself and travel up and down the rivers. These people proved highly conscious of their position and of their economic importance and they took the initiative of launching strikes without any trade union leadership at all. We therefore decided to concentrate all our work on this group. This gave excellent results and this group soon came to form a kind of nucleus which influenced the attitudes of other wage-earning groups in the towns—workers proper and drivers, who form two other important groups. Moreover, If I may put it this way, we thus found our little proletariat.

We also looked for intellectuals, but there were none, because the Portuguese did not educate people. In any case, what is an intellectual in our country? It could probably be someone who knew the general situation very well, who had some knowledge, not profound theoretical knowledge, but concrete knowledge of the country itself and of its life, as well as of our enemy. We, the people I have talked about, the engineers, doctors, bank clerks and so on, joined together to form a group of *interlocuteurs valables*.

There was also this other group of people in the towns,

which we have been unable to classify precisely, which was still closely connected to the rural areas and contained people who spoke almost all the languages that are used in Guinea. They knew all the customs of the rural areas while at the same time possessing a solid knowledge of the European urban centres. They also had a certain degree of self-confidence, they knew how to read and write (which makes a person an intellectual in our country) and so we concentrated our work on these people and immediately started giving them some preparatory training.

We were faced with another difficult problem: we realised that we needed to have people with a mentality which could transcend the context of the national liberation struggle, and so we prepared a number of cadres from the group I have just mentioned, some from the people employed in commerce and other wage-earners, and even some peasants, so that they could acquire what you might call a working class mentality. You may think this is absurd—in any case it is very difficult; in order for there to be a working class mentality the material conditions of the working class should exist, a working class should exist. In fact we managed to inculcate these ideas into a large number of people—the kind of ideas, that it, which there would be if there were a working class. We trained about 1,000 cadres at our party school in Conakry, in fact for about two years this was about all we did outside the country. When these cadres returned to the rural areas they inculcated a certain mentality into the peasants and it is among these cadres that we have chosen the people who are now leading the struggle; we are not a Communist party or a Marxist-Leninist party but the people now leading the peasants in the struggle in Guinea are mostly from the urban milieux and connected with the urban wage-earning group. When I hear that only the peasantry can lead the struggle, am I supposed to think we have made a mistake? All I can say is that at the moment our struggle is going well.

There are all sorts of other generalisations of a political nature, like this generalisation about the peasantry, which keeps on cropping up. There are a number of key words and concepts, there is a certain conditioning in the reasoning of our European friends: for example, when someone thinks, "revolution", he thinks of the bourgeoisie falling, etc.; when someone thinks "party", he forgets many things. Yesterday a friend asked me a number of questions about our party and several times I had to say to him, "but it isn't a European party"; the concept of a party and the creation of parties did not occur spontaneously in Europe, they resulted from a long process of class struggle. When we in Africa think of creating a party now we find ourselves in very different conditions from those in which parties appeared as historico-social phenomena in Europe. This has a number of consequences, so when you think "party", "single party", etc. you must connect all these things up with the history and conditions of Africa.

A rigorous historical approach is similarly needed when examining another problem related to this—how can the underdeveloped countries evolve towards revolution, towards socialism? There is a preconception held by many people, even on the left, that imperialism made us enter history at the moment when it began its adventure in our countries. This preconception must be denounced: for somebody on the left, and for Marxists in particular, history obviously means the class struggle. Our opinion is exactly the contrary. We consider that when imperialism arrived in Guinea it made us leave history—our history. We agree that history in our country is the result of class struggle, but we have our own class struggles in our own country; the moment imperialism arrived and colonialism arrived, it made us leave our history and enter another history. Obviously we agree that the class struggle has continued, but it has continued in a very different way: our whole people is struggling against the ruling class of the imperialist countries, and this gives a completely different aspect to the historical evolution of our country. Somebody has asked which class is the 'agent' of history; here a distinction must be drawn between colonial history and our history as human societies; as a dominated people we only present an ensemble vis-à-vis the oppressor. Each of our peoples or groups of peoples has been subjected to different influences by the colonisers; when there is a developed national consciousness one may ask which social stratum is the agent of history, of colonial history; which is the stratum which will be able to take power into its hands when it emerges from colonial history? Our answer is that it is *all* the social strata, if the people who have carried out the national revolution (ie the struggle against colonialism) have worked well, since unity of all the social strata is a prerequisite for the success of the national liberation struggle. As we see it, in colonial conditions no one stratum can succeed in the struggle for national liberation on its own, and therefore it is all the strata of society which are the agents of history. This brings us to what should be a void—but in fact it is not. What commands history in colonial conditions is not the class struggle. I do not mean that the class struggle in Guinea stopped completely during the colonial period; it continued, but in a muted way. In the colonial period it is the colonial state which commands history.

Our problem is to see who is capable of taking control of the state apparatus when the colonial power is destroyed. In Guinea the peasants cannot read or write, they have almost no relations with the colonial forces during the colonial period except for paying taxes, which is done indirectly. The working class hardly exists as a defined class, it is just an embryo. There is no *economically viable* bourgeoisie because imperialism prevented it being created. What there is is a stratum of people in the service of imperialism who have learned how to manipulate the apparatus of the state—the African petty bourgeoisie: this is the only stratum capable of controlling or even utilising the instruments which the colonial state used against our people. So we come to the conclusion that in colonial conditions it is the petty bourgeoisie which is the inheritor of state power (though I wish we could be wrong). The moment national liberation comes and the petty bourgeoisie takes power we enter, or rather return to history, and thus the internal contradictions break out again.

When this happens, and particularly as things are now, there will be powerful external contradictions conditioning the internal situation, and not just internal contradictions as before. What attitude can the petty bourgeoisie adopt? Obviously people on the left will call for the revolution; the right will call for the 'non-revolution', ie a capitalist road or something like that. The petty bourgeoisie can either ally itself with imperialism and the reactionary strata in its own country to try and preserve itself as a petty bourgeoisie or ally itself with the workers and peasants, who must themselves take power or control to make the revolution. We must be very clear exactly what we are asking the petty bourgeoisie to do. Are we asking it to commit suicide? Because if there is a revolution, then the petty bourgeoisie will have to abandon power to the workers and the peasants and cease to exist qua petty bourgeoisie. For a revolution to take place depends on the nature of the party (and its size), the character of the struggle which led up to liberation, whether there was an armed struggle, what the nature of this armed struggle was and how it developed and, of course, on the nature of the state.

Here I would like to say something about the position of our friends on the left; if a petty bourgeoisie comes to power, they obviously demand of it that it carry out a revolution. But the important thing is whether they took the precaution of analysing the position of the petty bourgeoisie during the struggle; did they examine its nature, see how it worked, see what instruments it used and see whether this bourgeoisie committed itself with the left to carrying out a revolution, before the liberation? As you can see, it is the struggle in the underdeveloped countries which endows the petty bourgeoisie with a function; in the capitalist countries the petty bourgeoisie is only a stratum which serves, it does not determine the historical orientation of the country; it merely allies itself with one group or another. So that to hope that the petty bourgeoisie will just carry out a revolution when it comes to power in an underdeveloped country is to hope for a miracle, although it is true that it *could* do this.

This connects with the problem of the true nature of the national liberation struggle. In Guinea, as in other countries, the implantation of imperialism by force and the presence of the colonial system considerably altered the historical conditions and aroused a response—the national liberation struggle—which is generally considered a revolutionary trend; but this is something which I think needs further examination. I should like to formulate this question: is the national liberation movement something which has simply emerged from within our country, is it a result of the internal contradictions created by the presence of colonialism, or are there external factors which have determined it? And here we have some reservations; in fact I would even go so far as to ask whether, given the advance of socialism in the world, the national liberation movement is not an imperialist initiative. Is the judicial institution which serves as a reference for the right of all peoples to struggle to free themselves a product of the peoples who are trying to liberate themselves? Was it created by the socialist countries who are our historical associates? It is signed by the imperialist countries, it is the imperialist countries who have recognised the right of all peoples to national independence, so I ask myself whether we may not be considering as an initiative of our people what is in fact an initiative of the enemy? Even Portugal, which is using napalm bombs against our people in Guinea, signed the declaration of the right of all peoples to independence. One may well ask oneself why they were so mad as to do something which goes against their own interests—and whether or not it was partly forced on them, the real point is that they signed it. This is where we think there is something wrong with the simple interpretation of the national liberation movement as a revolutionary trend. The objective of the imperialist countries was to prevent the enlargement of the socialist camp, to liberate the reactionary forces in our countries which were being stifled by colonialism and to enable these forces to ally themselves with the international bourgeoisie. The fundamental objective was to create a bourgeoisie where one did not exist, in order specifically to strengthen the imperialist and the capitalist camp. This rise of the bourgeoisie in the new countries, far from being at all surprising, should be considered absolutely normal, it is something that has to be faced by all those struggling against imperialism. We are therefore faced with the problem of deciding whether to engage in an out and out struggle against the bourgeoisie right from the start or whether to try and make an alliance with the national bourgeoisie, to try to deepen the absolutely necessary contradiction between the national bourgeoisie and the international bourgeoisie which has promoted the national bourgeoisie to the position it holds.

To return to the question of the nature of the petty bourgeoisie and the role it can play after the liberation, I should like to put a question to you. What would you have thought if Fidel Castro had come to terms with the Americans? Is this possible or not? Is it possible or impossible that the Cuban petty bourgeoisie, which set the Cuban people marching towards revolution, might have come to terms with the Americans? I think this helps to clarify the character of the revolutionary petty bourgeoisie. If I may put it this way, I think one thing that can be said is this: the revolutionary petty bourgeoisie is honest; ie in spite of all the hostile conditions, it remains identified with the fundamental interests of the popular masses. To do this it may have to commit suicide, but it will not lose; by sacrificing itself it can reincarnate itself, but in the condition of workers or peasants. In speaking of honesty I am not trying to establish moral criteria for judging the role of the petty bourgeoisie when it is in power; what I mean by honesty, in a political context, is total commitment and total identification with the toiling masses.

Again, the role of the petty bourgeoisie ties up with the possible social and political transformations that can be effected after liberation. We have heard a great deal about the state of national democracy, but although we have made every effort we have thus far been unable to understand what this means; even so, we should like to know what it is all about, as we want to know what we are going to do when we have driven out the Portuguese. Likewise, we have to face the question whether or not socialism can be established immediately after the liberation. This depends on the instruments used to effect the transition to socialism; the essential factor is the nature of the state, bearing in mind that after the liberation there will be people controlling the police, the prisons, the army and so on, and a great deal depends on who they are and what they try to do with these instruments. Thus we return again to the problem of which class is the agent of history and who are the inheritors of the colonial state in our specific conditions.

I mentioned briefly earlier the question of the attitude of the European left towards the underdeveloped countries, in which there is a good deal of criticism and a good deal of optimism. The criticism reminds me of a story about some lions: there is a group of lions who are shown a picture of a lion lying on the ground and a man holding a gun with his foot on the lion (as everybody knows the lion is proud of being king of the jungle); one of the lions looks at the picture and says, "if only we lions could paint". If one of the leaders of one of the new African countries could take time off from the terrible problems in his own country and become a critic of the European left and say all he had to say about the retreat of the revolution in Europe, of a certain apathy in some European countries and of the false hopes which we have all had in certain European groups . . . .

What really interests us here is neocolonialism. After the Second World War, imperialism entered on a new phase: on the one hand, it worked out the new policy of aid, ie granted independence to the occupied countries plus 'aid' and, on the other hand, concentrated on preferential investment in the European countries; this was, above all, an attempt at rationalising imperialism. Even if it has not yet provoked reactions of a nationalist kind in the European countries, we are convinced that it will soon do so. As we see it, neocolonialism (which we may call rationalised imperialism) is more a defeat for the international working class than for the colonised peoples. Neocolonialism is at work on two fronts—in Europe as well as in the underdeveloped countries. Its current framework in the underdeveloped countries is the policy of aid, and one of the essential aims of this policy is to create a false bourgeoisie to put a brake on the revolution and to enlarge the possibilities of the petty bourgeoisie as a neutraliser of the revolution; at the same time it invests capital in France, Italy, Belgium, England and so on. In our opinion the aim of this is to stimulate the growth of a workers' aristocracy, to enlarge the field of action of the petty bourgeoisie so as to block the revolution. In our opinion it is under this aspect that neocolonialism and the relations between the international working class movement and our movements must be analysed.

If there have ever been any doubts about the close relations between our struggle and the struggle of the international working class movement, neocolonialism has proved that there need not be any. Obviously I don't think it is possible to forge closer relations between the peasantry in Guinea and the working class movement in Europe; what we must do first is try and forge closer links between the peasant movement and the wage-earners' movement in our own country. The example of Latin America gives you a good idea of the limits on closer relations; in Latin America you have an old neocolonial situation and a chance to see clearly the relations between the North American proletariat and the Latin American masses. Other examples could be found nearer home.

There is, however, another aspect I should like to raise and that is that the European left has an intellectual responsibility to study the concrete conditions in our country and help us in this way, as we have very little documentation, very few intellectuals, very little chance to do this kind of work ourselves, and yet it is of key importance: this is a major contribution you can make. Another thing you can do is to support the really revolutionary national liberation movements by all possible means. You must analyse and study these movements and combat in Europe, by all possible means, everything which can be used to further the repression against our peoples. I refer especially to the sale of arms. I should like to say to our Italian friends that we have captured a lot of Italian arms from the Portuguese, not to mention French arms, of course. Moreover, you must unmask courageously all the national liberation movements which are under the thumb of imperialism. People whisper that so-and-so is an American agent, but nobody in the European left has taken a violent and open attitude against these people; it is we ourselves who have to try and denounce these people, who are sometimes even those accepted by the rest of Africa, and this creates a lot of trouble for us.

I think that the left and the international working class movement should confront those states which claim to be socialist with their responsibilities; this does not of course, mean cutting off all their possibilities of action, but it does mean denouncing all those states which are neo-colonialist.

To end up with, I should just like to make one last point about solidarity between the international working class movement and our national liberation struggle. There are two alternatives: either we admit that there really is a struggle against imperialism which interests everybody, or we deny it. If, as would seem from all the evidence, imperialism exists and is trying simultaneously to dominate the working class in all the advanced countries and smother the national liberation movements in all the underdeveloped countries, then there is only one enemy against whom we are fighting. If we are fighting together, then I think the main aspect of our solidarity is extremely simple: it is to fight—I don't think there is any need to discuss this very much. We are struggling in Guinea with guns in our hands, you must struggle in your countries as well—I don't say with guns in your hands, I'm not going to tell you how to struggle, that's your business; but you must find the best means and the best forms of fighting against our common enemy: this is the best form of solidarity.

There are, of course, other secondary forms of solidarity: publishing material, sending medicine, etc; I can guarantee you that if tomorrow we make a breakthrough and you are engaged in an armed struggle against imperialism in Europe we will send you some medicine too.

The Nationalist Movements of the Portuguese Colonies

Opening address at the CONCP Conference held in Dar Es-Salaam, 1965.

Dear comrades and friends: I am going to tell you very simply and as briefly as possible about our position, our situation and, if you like, our options. A brief analysis we would like to make objectively and without passion. If we do not forget the historical perspectives of the major events in the life of humanity, if, while maintaining due respect for all philosophies, we do not forget that the world is the creation of man himself, then colonialism can be considered as the paralysis or deviation or even the halting of the history of one people in favour of the acceleration of the historical development of other peoples.

This is why, when speaking of Portuguese colonialism, we should not isolate it from the totality of the other phenomena which have characterised the life of humanity since the industrial revolution, from the rise of capitalism to the Second World War. This is why, when speaking of our struggle, we should not isolate it from the totality of the phenomena which have characterised the life of humanity, in particular in Africa since the Second World War.

I remember that period very well. We are getting old. I remember very well how some of us, still students, got together in Lisbon, influenced by the currents which were shaking the world, and began to discuss one day what could today be called the re-Africanisation of our minds. Yes, some of those people are here in this hall. And that, dear friends, is a striking victory against the retrograde forces of Portuguese colonialism. You have among you here Agostinho Neto, Mario de Andrade, Marcelino Dos Santos, you have among you Vasco Cabral and Dr. Mondlane. All of us, in Lisbon, some permanently, others temporarily, began this march, this already long march towards the liberation of our peoples.

In the second world war millions of men, women and children, millions of soldiers gave their lives for an ideal, an ideal of democracy, freedom, progress and a just life for all men. Clearly, we know that the second world war produced fundamental contradictions within the imperialist camp itself. But we also know that one of the fundamental objectives of that war started by Hitler and his horde was the destruction of the socialist camp about to be born.

We know too that in the heart of every man fighting in that war there was hope, the hope for a better world. It was that hope which touched us all, making us fighters for the freedom of our peoples. But we must state openly that equally if not more so, it is the concrete conditions of the life of our peoples—misery, ignorance, suffering of every kind, the complete negation of our most elementary rights—which have dictated our firm position against Portuguese colonialism and, consequently, against all injustice in the world.

We had many meetings, we created many organisations. I am going to recall just one of those organisations: the Anti-Colonialist Movement, MAC.

One day we will publish the famous—for us very famous and historic—manifesto of the MAC, in which you will certainly find the preface to our struggle, the general line of the struggle which we are victoriously waging today against Portuguese colonialism. We are fighting against Portuguese colonialism. In any struggle it is of fundamental importance to define clearly who we are, and who is the enemy. We, the peoples of the Portuguese colonies, are African peoples, of this Africa ensnared by imperialism and colonialism for decades and even in some cases for centuries. We are from the part of Africa which the imperialists call Black Africa. Yes, we are Black. But we are men like all other men. Our countries are economically backward. Our peoples are at a specific historical stage characterised by this backward condition of our economy. We must be conscious of this. We are African peoples, we have not invented many things, we do not possess today the special weapons which others possess, we have no big factories, we don't even have for our children the toys which other children have, but we do have our own hearts, our own heads, our own history. It is this history which the colonialists have taken from us. The colonialists usually say that it was they who brought us into history: today we show that this is not so. They made us leave history, our history, to follow them, right at the back, to follow the progress of their history. Today, in taking up arms to liberate ourselves, in following the example of other peoples who have taken up arms to liberate themselves, we want to return to our history, on our own feet, by our own means and through our own sacrifices. We, peoples of Africa, who are fighting against Portuguese colonialism, have suffered under very special conditions, because for the past forty years we have been under the domination of a fascist regime.

Who is this enemy who dominates us, stubbornly scorning all laws, all international legality and morality? This enemy is not the Portuguese people, nor even Portugal itself: for us, fighting for the freedom of the Portuguese colonies, the enemy is Portuguese colonialism, represented by the colonial-fascist government of Portugal. But obviously a government is also to some extent the result of the historical, geographical and economic conditions of the country which it governs. Portugal is an economically backward country, in which about 50% of the population is illiterate, a country which you will find at the bottom of all the statistical tables of Europe. This is not the fault of the Portuguese people who, at a certain time in history, showed their valour, their courage and their capacity, and who even today possess capable sons, just sons, sons who also want to regain freedom and happiness for their people.

Portugal is a country in no position at all to dominate any other country. Portugal came to our countries proclaiming it came in the service of God and in the service of civilisation. Today we reply with arms in our hands: whichever God is with the Portuguese colonialists, whichever civilisation the Portuguese colonialists represent, we are going to destroy them because we are going to destroy every sort of foreign domination in our countries.

I will not go into detail about the characteristics of Portuguese colonialism. The main characteristic of present-day Portuguese colonialism is a very simple fact: Portuguese colonialism, or if you prefer the Portuguese economic infrastructure, cannot allow itself the luxury of being neo-colonialist. This enables us to understand the whole attitude, all the stubbornness of Portuguese colonialism towards our peoples. If Portugal was economically advanced, if Portugal could be classified as a developed country, we should surely not be at war with Portugal today.

Many people criticise Salazar and say bad things about him. He is a man like any other. He has many failings, he is a fascist, we hate him, but we are not fighting against Salazar, we are fighting against the Portuguese colonial system. We don't dream that when Salazar disappears Portuguese colonialism will disappear.

Our national liberation struggle has a great significance both for Africa and for the world. We are in the process of proving that peoples such as ours—economically backward, living sometimes almost naked in the bush, not knowing how to read or write, not having even the most elementary knowledge of modern technology—are capable, by means of their sacrifices and efforts, of beating an enemy who is not only more advanced from a technological point of view but also supported by the powerful forces of world imperialism. Thus before the world and before Africa we ask: were the Portuguese right when they claimed that we were un-civilised peoples, peoples without culture? We ask: what is the most striking manifestation of civilisation and culture if not that shown by a people which takes up arms to defend its right to life, to progress, to work and to happiness?

We, the national liberation movements joined in the CONCP, should be conscious of the fact that our armed struggle is only one aspect of the general struggle of the oppressed peoples against imperialism, of man's struggle for dignity, freedom and progress. We should consider ourselves as soldiers, often anonymous, but soldiers of humanity in the vast front of struggle in Africa today.

We must also define clearly our position in relation to our people, in relation to Africa, and in relation to the world. We of the CONCP are committed to our peoples, we are fighting for the complete liberation of our peoples, but we are not fighting simply in order to hoist a flag in our countries and to have a national anthem. We of the CONCP are fighting so that insults may no longer rule our countries, martyred and scorned for centuries, so that our peoples may never more be exploited by imperialists—not only by Europeans, not only by people with white skin, because we do not confuse exploitation or exploiters with the colour of men's skins; we do not want any exploitation in our countries, not even by black people. . . .

In Africa we are all for the complete liberation of the African continent from the colonial yoke, for we know that colonialism is an instrument of imperialism. So we want to see all manifestations of imperialism totally wiped out on the soil of Africa; in the CONCP we are fiercely opposed to neo-colonialism, whatever its form. Our struggle is not only against Portuguese colonialism; in the framework of our struggle we want to make the most effective contribution possible to the complete elimination of foreign domination in our continent.

In Africa we are for African unity, but we are for African unity in favour of the African peoples. We consider unity to be a means, not an end. Unity can reinforce and accelerate the reaching of ends, but we must not betray the end. That is why we are not in such a great hurry to achieve African unity. We know that it will come, step by step, as a result of the fruitful efforts of the African peoples. It will come at the service of Africa and of humanity. In the CONCP we are firmly convinced that making full use of the riches of our continent, of its human, moral and cultural capacities, will contribute to creating a rich human species, which in turn will make a considerable contribution to humanity. But we do not want the dream of this end to betray in its achievement the interests of each African people. We, for example, in Guinea and Cabo Verde, openly declare in our Party's programme that we are willing to join any African people, with only one condition: that the gains made by our people in the liberation struggle, the economic and social gains and the justice which we seek and are achieving little by little, should not be compromised by unity with other peoples. That is our only condition for unity.

In Africa, we are for an African policy which seeks to defend first and foremost the interests of the African peoples, of each African country, but also for a policy which does not, at any time, forget the interests of the world, of all humanity. We are for a policy of peace in Africa and of fraternal collaboration with all the peoples of the world.

On an international level, we in the CONCP practice a policy of non-alignment. But for us non-alignment does not mean turning one's back on the fundamental problems of humanity and of justice. Non-alignment for us means not aligning ourselves with blocs, not aligning ourselves with the decisions of others. We reserve the right to make our own decisions, and if by chance our choices and decisions coincide with those of others, that is not our fault.

We are for the policy of non-alignment, but we consider ourselves to be deeply committed to our people and committed to every just cause in the world. We see ourselves as part of a vast front of struggle for the good of humanity. You understand that we are struggling first and foremost for our own peoples. That is our task in this front of struggle. This involves the whole problem of solidarity. We in the CONCP are fiercely in solidarity with every just cause. That is why our hearts, in FRELIMO, in MPLA, in the PAIGC, in the CLSTP, in all the mass organisations affiliated to the CONCP, beat in unison with the hearts of our brothers in Vietnam who are giving us a shining example by facing the most shameful and unjustifiable aggression of the U.S. imperialists against the peaceful people of Vietnam. Our hearts are equally with our brothers in the Congo who, in the bush of that vast and rich African country are seeking to resolve their problems in the face of imperialist aggression and of the manoeuvres of imperialism through their puppets. That is why we of the CONCP proclaim loud and clear that we are against Tshombe, against all the Tshombes of Africa. Our hearts are also with our brothers in Cuba, who have shown that even when surrounded by the sea, a people is capable of taking up arms and successfully defending its fundamental interests and of deciding its own destiny. We are with the Blacks of North America, we are with them in the streets of Los Angeles, and when they are deprived of all possibility of life, we suffer with them.

We are with the refugees, the martyrised refugees of Palestine, who have been tricked and driven from their own homeland by the manoeuvres of imperialism. We are on the side of the Palestinian refugees and we support whole-heartedly all that the sons of Palestine are doing to liberate their country, and we fully support the Arab and African countries in general in helping the Palestinian people to recover their dignity, their independence and their right to live. We are also with the peoples of Southern Arabia, of so-called 'French Somaliland, of so-called 'Spanish' Guinea, and we are also most seriously and painfully with our brothers in South Africa who are facing the most barbarous racial discrimination. We are absolutely certain that the development of the struggle in the Portuguese colonies, and the victory we are winning each day over Portuguese colonialism is an effective contribution to the elimination of the vile, shameful regime of racial discrimination, of apartheid in South Africa. And we are also certain that peoples like that of Angola, that of Mozambique and ourselves in Guinea and Cabo Verde, far from South Africa, will soon, very soon we hope, be able to play a very important role in the final elimination of that last bastion of imperialism and racism in Africa, South Africa.

We strongly support all just causes in the world, but we are also reinforced by the support of others. We receive concrete assistance from many people, from many friends, from many brothers. We accept every sort of assistance, from wherever it comes, but we never ask anybody for the assistance which we need. We just wait for whatever assistance each person or people can give to our struggle. Those are our *ethics* of assistance.

It is our duty to state here, loud and clear, that we have firm allies in the socialist countries. We know that all the African peoples are our brothers. Our struggle is their struggle. Every drop of blood that falls in our countries falls also from the body and heart of our brothers, these African peoples. But we also know that since the socialist revolution and the events of the second world war, the face of the world has been definitely changed. A socialist camp has arisen in the world. This has radically changed the balance of power, and this socialist camp is today showing itself fully conscious of its duties, international and historic, but not moral, since the peoples of the socialist countries have never exploited the colonised peoples. They are showing themselves conscious of their duty, and this is why I have the honour of telling you openly here that we are receiving substantial and effective aid from these countries, which is reinforcing the aid which we receive from our African brothers. If there are people who don't like to hear this, let them come and help us in our struggle too. But they can be sure that we are proud of our own sovereignty.

And what are they doing, these people who don't like to

hear us saying that the socialist countries are helping us? They are helping Portugal, the fascist-colonial government of Salazar. Everybody knows today that Portugal, the Portuguese government, if it could not count on the assistance of its NATO allies, would not be able to carry on fighting against us. But we must state clearly what NATO means. Yes, we know: NATO is a military bloc which defends the interests of the West, of Western civilisation, etc. . . . That is not what we wish to discuss. NATO is concrete countries, concrete governments and states. NATO is the USA. We have captured in our country many US weapons. NATO is the Federal Republic of Germany. We have a lot of Mauser rifles taken from Portuguese soldiers. NATO, for the time being at least, is France. In our country there are Alouette helicopters. NATO is, too, to a certain extent, the government of that heroic people which has given so many examples of love of freedom, the Italian people. Yes, we have captured from the Portuguese machine-guns and grenades made in Italy.

Portugal has other allies too: South Africa, Mr Smith of Southern Rhodesia, the government of Franco, and other obscure allies who hide their faces because of the shame which this represents. But all this assistance which the Salazar government receives to kill our people and burn our villages in Angola, Mozambique, Guinea, Cabo Verde and Sao Tomé has been incapable of stopping our national liberation struggle. On the contrary, our forces become stronger each day. And why? Because our strength is the strength of justice, progress and history; and justice, progress and history belong to the people. Because our fundamental strength is the strength of the people. It is our peoples who support our organisations, it is our peoples who are making sacrifices every day to supply all the needs of our struggle. It is our peoples who guarantee the future and the certainty of our victory.

In the perspective of our struggle, the place of this conference is clear. We must strengthen our unity, not only within each country but also among ourselves, as peoples of the Portuguese colonies. The CONCP has a very special significance for us. We have the same colonial past, we have all learned to speak and write Portuguese, but we have an even greater, and perhaps even more historic, strength: the fact that we began the struggle together. It is the struggle which makes comrades, which makes companions, for the present and for the future. The CONCP is for us a fundamental force in the struggle. The CONCP is in the heart of every fighter in our country, in Mozambique and Angola. The CONCP must also be an example, of which we are proud, to the peoples of Africa. Because in this glorious struggle against imperialism and colonialism in

Africa, we are the first colonies to have joined together to discuss together, to plan together, to study together the problems concerning the development of their struggle. This is surely a very interesting contribution to the history of Africa and to the history of our peoples.

Africa assists us, yes. There are some African countries which assist us as much as they can, directly, bilaterally. But in our opinion Africa does not assist us enough. In our opinion Africa could help us much more, if Africa could understand the value and importance of our struggle against Portuguese colonialism; so we hope that on the experience of the two years since Addis Ababa, the next summit conference of African heads-of-state will take concrete steps to effectively reinforce Africa's aid to the combatants of Guinea, Cabo Verde, San Tomé, Mozambique and Angola. Equally, our friends in the world, and in particular our friends the socialist countries, will surely be aware that the development of our struggle involves the development of their fraternal assistance; and we are sure that the socialist countries and the progressive forces of the West will develop their assistance and their political, moral and material support for our struggle as this struggle itself develops.

To finish, I would like to simply say this: in our country, in Guinea and the Cabo Verde Islands, the colonialist troops are pulling further back each day. Today if we want to fight the colonialist troops, we have to go to them, we have to fight them in their barracks. But we must go there because we must eliminate Portuguese colonialism from our country. We are sure, dear friends, that it will soon be the same in Mozambique—and it is already happening in certain areas there. It will be the same in Angola—and it is already happening in Cabinda. The Portuguese colonialists are beginning to be afraid of us. They sense now that they are lost, but I assure you that if they were present here today—it's a pity they don't have any agents here—seeing us, hearing all the delegations speak, seeing all these people, seeing the fraternal welcome which the government of Tanzania has given us, the fear of the Portuguese colonialists would be even greater. But comrades and brothers, let us go forward, weapons in hand, everywhere where there is a Portuguese colonialist. Let us go forward and destroy him and liberate our countries quickly from the retrograde forces of Portuguese colonialism. But let us prepare ourselves too, each day, and be vigilant, so as not to allow a new form of colonialism to be established in our countries, so as not to allow in our countries any form of imperialism, so as not to allow neo-colonialism, already a cancerous growth in certain parts of Africa and of the world, to reach our own countries.

Tell no lies
Claim no easy victories . . .

Extracts from Party directive 1965

Always bear in mind that the people are not fighting for ideas, for the things in anyone's head. They are fighting to win material benefits, to live better and in peace, to see their lives go forward, to guarantee the future of their children . . . .

We should recognise as a matter of conscience that there have been many faults and errors in our action whether political or military: an important number of things we should have done we have not done at the right times, or not done at all.

In various regions—and indeed everywhere in a general sense—political work among the people and among our armed forces has not been done appropriately: responsible workers have not carried or have not been able to carry through the work of mobilization, formation and political organisation defined by the party leadership. Here and there, even among responsible workers, there has been a marked tendency to let things slide . . . and even a certain demobilisation which has not been fought and eliminated . . . .

On the military plane, many plans and objectives established by the Party leadership have not been achieved. With the means we have, we could do much more and better. Some responsible workers have misunderstood the functions of the army and guerilla forces, have not made good co-ordination between these two and, in certain cases, have allowed themselves to be influenced by preoccupation with the defence of our positions, ignoring the fact that, for us, attack is the best means of defence . . . .

And with all this as a proof of insufficient political work among our armed forces, there has appeared a certain attitude of 'militarism' which has caused some fighters and even some leaders to forget the fact that we are *armed militants* and not *militarists*. This tendency must be urgently fought and eliminated within the army . . . .

If ten men go to a ricefield and do the day's work of eight, there's no reason to be satisfied. It's the same in battle. Ten men fight like eight; that's not enough . . . . One can always do more. Some people get used to the war, and once you get used to a thing it's the end: you get a bullet up the spout of your gun and you walk around. You hear the motor on the river and you don't use the bazooka that you have, so the

Portuguese boats pass unharmed. Let me repeat: one can do more. We have to throw the Portuguese out . . . .

. . . Create schools and spread education in all liberated areas. Select young people between 14 and 20, those who have at least completed their fourth year, for further training. Oppose without violence all prejudicial customs, the negative aspects of the beliefs and traditions of our people. Oblige every responsible and educated member of our Party to work daily for the improvement of their cultural formation . . . .

Oppose among the young, especially those over 20, the mania for leaving the country so as to study elsewhere, the blind ambition to acquire a degree, the complex of inferiority and the mistaken idea which leads to the belief that those who study or take courses will thereby become privileged in our country tomorrow . . . . But also oppose any ill will towards those who study or wish to study—the complex that students will be parasites or future saboteurs of the Party . . . .

In the liberated areas, do everything possible to normalise the political life of the people. Section committees of the Party *(tabanca* committees), zonal committees, regional committees, must be consolidated and function normally. Frequent meetings must be held to explain to the population what is happening in the struggle, what the Party is endeavouring to do at any given moment, and what the criminal intentions of the enemy may be.

In regions still occupied by the enemy, reinforce clandestine work, the mobilisation and organisation of the populations, and the preparation of militants for action and support of our fighters . . . .

Develop political work in our armed forces, whether regular or guerilla, wherever they may be. Hold frequent meetings. Demand serious political work from political commissars. Start political committees, formed by the political commissar and commander of each unit in the regular army.

Oppose tendencies to militarism and make each fighter an exemplary militant of our Party.

Educate ourselves, educate other people, the population in general, to fight fear and ignorance, to eliminate little by little the subjection to nature and natural forces which our economy has not yet mastered. Convince little by little, in particular the militants of the Party, that we shall end by conquering the fear of nature, and that man is the strongest force in nature.

Demand from responsible Party members that they dedicate themselves seriously to study, that they interest themselves in the things and problems of our daily life and struggle in their fundamental and essential aspect, and not simply in their appearance . . . . Learn from life, learn from our people, learn from books, learn from the experience of others. Never stop learning.

Responsible members must take life seriously, conscious of their responsibilities, thoughtful about carrying them out, and with a comradeship based on work and duty done . . . . Nothing of this is incompatible with the joy of living, or with love for life and its amusements, or with confidence in the future and in our work . . . .

Reinforce political work and propaganda within the enemy's armed forces. Write posters, pamphlets, letters. Draw slogans on the roads. Establish cautious links with enemy personnel who want to contact us. Act audaciously and with great initiative in this way . . . . Do everything possible to help enemy soldiers to desert. Assure them of security so as to encourage their desertion. Carry out political work among Africans who are still in enemy service, whether civilian or military. Persuade these brothers to change direction so as to serve the Party within enemy ranks or desert with arms and ammunition to our units.

We must practice revolutionary democracy in every aspect of our Party life. Every responsible member must have the courage of his responsibilities, exacting from others a proper respect for his work and properly respecting the work of others. Hide nothing from the masses of our people. Tell no lies. Expose lies whenever they are told. Mask no difficulties, mistakes, failures. Claim no easy victories . . . .

These extracts were first published in English in Basil Davidson's *The Liberation of Guiné, aspects of an African revolution* (Penguin 1969)

The weapon of theory

Address delivered to the first Tricontinental Conference of the peoples of Asia, Africa and Latin America held in Havana in January 1966

If any of us came to Cuba with doubts in our mind about the solidity, strength, maturity and vitality of the Cuban Revolution, these doubts have been removed by what we have been able to see. Our hearts are now warmed by an unshakable certainty which gives us courage in the difficult but glorious struggle against the common enemy: no power in the world will be able to destroy this Cuban Revolution, which is creating in the countryside and in the towns not only a new life but also—and even more important—a New Man, fully conscious of his national, continental and international rights and duties. In every field of activity the Cuban people have made major progress during the last seven years, particularly in 1965, Year of Agriculture.

We believe that this constitutes a particular lesson for the national liberation movements, especially for those who want their national revolution to be a true revolution. Some people have not failed to note that a certain number of Cubans, albeit an insignificant minority, have not shared the joys and hopes of the celebrations for the seventh anniversary because they are against the Revolution. It is possible that others will not be present at the celebrations of the eighth anniversary, but we would like to state that we consider the 'open door' policy for enemies of the Revolution to be a lesson in courage, determination, humanity and confidence in the people, another political and moral victory over the enemy; and to those who are worried, in a spirit of friendship, about the dangers which may be involved in this exodus, we guarantee that we, the peoples of the countries of Africa, still completely dominated by Portuguese colonialism, are prepared to send to Cuba as many men and women as may be needed to compensate for the departure of those who for reasons of class or of inability to adapt have interests or attitudes which are incompatible with the interests of the Cuban people. Taking once again the formerly hard and tragic path of our ancestors (mainly from Guinea and Angola) who were taken to Cuba as slaves, we would come now as free men, as willing workers and Cuban patriots, to fulfil a productive function in this new, just and multi-racial society, and to help and defend with our own lives the victories of the Cuban people. Thus we would strengthen both all the bonds of history, blood and culture which unite our peoples with the Cuban people, and the spontaneous giving of oneself, the deep joy and infectious rhythm which make the construction of socialism in Cuba a new phenomenon for the world, a unique and, for many, unaccustomed event.

We are not going to use this platform to rail against imperialism. An African saying very common in our country says: "When your house is burning, it's no use beating the tom-toms." On a Tricontinental level, this means that we are not going to eliminate imperialism by shouting insults against it. For us, the best or worst shout against imperialism, whatever its form, is to take up arms and fight. This is what we are doing, and this is what we will go on doing until all foreign domination of our African homelands has been totally eliminated.

Our agenda includes subjects whose meaning and importance are beyond question and which show a fundamental preoccupation with *struggle*. We note, however, that one form of struggle which we consider to be fundamental has not been explicitly mentioned in this programme, although we are certain that it was present in the minds of those who drew up the programme. We refer here to *the struggle against our own weaknesses*. Obviously, other cases differ from that of Guinea; but our experience has shown us that in the general framework of daily struggle this battle against ourselves—no matter what difficulties the enemy may create—is the most difficult of all, whether for the present or the future of our peoples. This battle is the expression of the internal contradictions in the economic, social, cultural (and therefore historical) reality of each of our countries. We are convinced that any national or social revolution which is not based on knowledge of this fundamental reality runs grave risk of being condemned to failure.

When the African peoples say in their simple language that "no matter how hot the water from your well, it will not cook your rice", they express with singular simplicity a fundamental principle, not only of physics, but also of political science. We know that the development of a phenomenon in movement, whatever its external appearance, depends mainly on its internal characteristics. We also know that on the political level our own reality—however fine and attractive the reality of others may be—can only be transformed by detailed knowledge of it, by our own efforts, by our own sacrifices. It is useful to recall in this Tricontinental gathering, so rich in experience and example, that however great the similarity between our various cases and however identical our enemies, national liberation and social revolution are not exportable commodities; they are, and increasingly so every day, the outcome of local and national elaboration, more or less influenced by external factors (be they favourable or unfavourable) but essentially determined and formed by the historical reality of each people, and carried to success by the overcoming or correct solution of the internal contradictions between the various categories characterising this reality. The success of the Cuban revolution, taking place only 90 miles from the greatest imperialist and anti-socialist power of all time, seems to us, in its content and its way of evolution, to be a practical and conclusive illustration of the validity of this principle.

However we must recognise that we ourselves and the other liberation movements in general (referring here above all to the African experience) have not managed to pay sufficient attention to this important problem of our common struggle.

The ideological deficiency, not to say the total lack of ideology, within the national liberation movements—which is basically due to ignorance of the historical reality which these movements claim to transform—constitutes one of the greatest weaknesses of our struggle against imperialism, if not the greatest weakness of all. We believe, however, that a sufficient number of different experiences has already been accumulated to enable us to define a general line of thought and action with the aim of eliminating this deficiency. A full discussion of this subject could be useful, and would enable this conference to make a valuable contribution towards strengthening the present and future actions of the national liberation movements. This would be a concrete way of helping these movements, and in our opinion no less important than political support or financial assistance for arms and suchlike.

It is with the intention of making a contribution, however modest, to this debate that we present here our opinion of *the foundations and objectives of national liberation in relation to the social structure*. This opinion is the result of our own experiences of the struggle and of a critical appreciation of the experiences of others. To those who see in it a theoretical character, we would recall that every practice produces a theory, and that if it is true that a revolution can fail even though it be based on perfectly conceived theories, nobody has yet made a successful revolution without a revolutionary theory.

Those who affirm—in our case correctly—that the motive force of history is the class struggle would certainly agree to a revision of this affirmation to make it more precise and give it an even wider field of application if they had a better knowledge of the essential characteristics of certain colonised peoples, that is to say peoples dominated by imperialism. In fact in the general evolution of humanity and of each of the peoples of which it is composed, classes appear neither as a generalised and simultaneous phenomenon throughout the totality of these groups, nor as a finished, perfect, uniform and spontaneous whole. The definition of classes within one or several human groups is a fundamental consequence of the progressive development of the productive forces and of the characteristics of the distribution of the wealth produced by the group or usurped from others. That is to say that the socio-economic phenomenon 'class' is created and develops as a function of at least two essential and interdependent variables—the level of productive forces and the pattern of ownership of the means of production. This development takes place slowly, gradually and unevenly, by quantitative and generally imperceptible variations in the fundamental components; once a certain degree of accumulation is reached, this process then leads to a *qualitative jump,* characterised by the appearance of classes and of conflict between them.

Factors external to the socio-economic whole can influence, more or less significantly, the process of development of classes, accelerating it, slowing it down and even causing regressions. When, for whatever reason, the influence of these factors ceases, the process reassumes its independence and its rhythm is then determined not only by the specific internal characteristics of the whole, but also by the resultant of the effect produced in it by the temporary action of the external factors. On a strictly internal level the rhythm of the process may vary, but it remains continuous and progressive. Sudden progress is only possible as a function of violent alterations—mutations—in the level of productive forces or in the pattern of ownership. These violent transformations carried out within the process of development of classes, as a result of mutations in the level of productive forces or in the pattern of ownership, are generally called, in economic and political language, *revolutions.*

Clearly, however, the possibilities of this process are noticeably influenced by external factors, and particularly by the interaction of human groups. This interaction is considerably increased by the development of means of transport and communication which has created the modern world, eliminating the isolation of human groups within one area, of areas within one continent, and between continents. This development, characteristic of a long historical period which began with the invention of the first means of transport, was already more evident at the time of the Punic voyages and in the Greek colonisation, and was accentuated by maritime discoveries, the invention of the steam engine and the discovery of electricity. And in our own times, with the progressive domesticization of atomic energy it is possible to promise, if not to take men to the stars, at least to humanise the universe.

This leads us to pose the following question: does history begin only with the development of the phenomenon of 'class', and consequently of class struggle? To reply in the affirmative would be to place outside history the whole period of life of human groups from the discovery of hunting, and later of nomadic and sedentary agriculture, to the organisation of herds and the private appropriation of land. It would also be to consider—and this we refuse to accept—that various human groups in Africa, Asia and Latin America were living without history, or outside history, at the time when they were subjected to the yoke of imperialism. It would be to consider that the peoples of our countries, such as the Balantes of Guinea, the Coaniamas of Angola and the Macondes of Mozambique, are still living today—if we abstract the slight influence of colonialism to which they have been subjected—outside history, or that they have no history.

Our refusal, based as it is on concrete knowledge of the socio-economic reality of our countries and on the analysis of the process of development of the phenomenon 'class', as we have seen earlier, leads us to conclude that if class struggle is the motive force of history, it is so only in a specific historical period. This means that *before* the class struggle—and necessarily *after* it, since in this world there is no before without an after—one or several factors was and will be the motive force of history. It is not difficult to see that this factor in the history of each human group is the *mode of production*—the level of productive forces and the pattern of ownership—characteristic of that group. Furthermore, as we have seen, classes themselves, class struggle and their subsequent definition, are the result of the development of the productive forces in conjunction with the pattern of ownership of the means of production. It therefore seems correct to conclude that the level of productive forces, the essential determining element in the content and form of class struggle, is the true and permanent motive force of history.

If we accept this conclusion, then the doubts in our minds are cleared away. Because if on the one hand we can see that the existence of history before the class struggle is guaranteed, and thus avoid for some human groups in our countries—and perhaps in our continent—the sad position of being peoples without any history, then on the other hand we can see that history has continuity, even after the disappearance of class struggle or of classes themselves. And as it was not we who postulated—on a scientific basis—the fact of the disappearance of classes as a historical inevitability, we can feel satisfied at having reached this conclusion which, to a certain extent, re-establishes coherence and at the same time gives to those peoples who, like the people of Cuba, are building socialism, the agreeable certainty that they will not cease to have a history when they complete the process of elimination of the phenomenon of 'class' and class struggle within their socio-economic whole. Eternity is not of this world, but man will outlive classes and will continue to produce and make history, since he can never free himself from the burden of his needs, both of mind and of body, which are the basis of the development of the forces of production.

The foregoing, and the reality of our times, allow us to state that the history of one human group or of humanity goes through at least three stages. The first is characterised by a low level of productive forces—of man's domination over nature; the mode of production is of a rudimentary character, private appropriation of the means of production does not yet exist, there are no classes, nor, consequently, is there any class struggle. In the second stage, the increased level of productive forces leads to private appropriation of the means of production, progressively complicates the mode of production, provokes conflicts of interests within the socio-economic whole in movement, and makes possible the appearance of the phenomenon 'class' and hence of class struggle, the social expression of the contradiction in the economic field between the mode of production and private appropriation of the means of production. In the third stage, once a certain level of productive forces is reached, the elimination of private appropriation of the means of production is made possible, and is carried out, together with the elimination of the phenomenon 'class', and hence of class struggle; new and hitherto unknown forces in the historical process of the socio-economic whole are then unleashed.

In politico-economic language, the first stage would correspond to the communal agricultural and cattle-raising society, in which the social structure is horizontal, without any state; the second to feudal or assimilated agricultural or agro-industrial bourgeois societies, with a vertical social structure and a state; the third to socialist or communist societies, in which the economy is mainly, if not exclusively, industrial (since agriculture itself becomes a form of industry) and in which the state tends to progressively disappear, or actually disappears, and where the social structure returns to horizontality, at a higher level of productive forces, social relations and appreciation of human values.

At the level of humanity or of part of humanity (human

groups within one area, of one or several continents) these three stages (or two of them) can be simultaneous, as is shown as much by the present as by the past. This is a result of the uneven development of human societies, whether caused by internal reasons or by one or more external factors exerting an accelerating or slowing-down influence on their evolution. On the other hand, in the historical process of a given socio-economic whole each of the above-mentioned stages contains, once a certain level of transformation is reached, the seeds of the following stage.

We should also note that in the present phase of the life of humanity, and for a given socio-economic whole, the time sequence of the three characteristic stages is not indispensable. Whatever its level of productive forces and present social structure, a society can pass rapidly through the defined stages appropriate to the concrete local realities (both historical and human) and reach a higher stage of existence. This progress depends on the concrete possibilities of development of the society's productive forces and is governed mainly by the nature of the political power ruling the society, that is to say, by the type of state or, if one likes, by the character of the dominant class or classes within the society.

A more detailed analysis would show that the possibility of such a jump in the historical process arises mainly, in the economic field, from the power of the means available to man at the time for dominating nature, and, in the political field, from the new event which has radically changed the face of the world and the development of history, *the creation of socialist states.*

Thus we see that our peoples have their own history regardless of the stage of their economic development. When they were subjected to imperialist domination, the historical process of each of our peoples (or of the human groups of which they are composed) was subjected to the violent action of an external factor. This action—the impact of imperialism on our societies—could not fail to influence the process of development of the productive forces in our countries and the social structures of our countries, as well as the content and form of our national liberation struggles.

But we also see that in the historical context of the development of these struggles, our peoples have the concrete possibility of going from their present situation of exploitation and underdevelopment to a new stage of their historical process which can lead them to a higher form of economic, social and cultural existence.

The political statement drawn up by the international preparatory committee of this conference, for which we reaffirm our complete support, placed imperialism, by clear and succinct analysis, in its economic context and historical co-ordinates. We will not repeat here what has already been said in the assembly. We will simply state that imperialism can be defined as a worldwide expression of the search for profits and the ever-increasing accumulation of *surplus value* by monopoly financial capital, centred in two parts of the world; first in Europe, and then in North America. And if we wish to place the fact of imperialism within the general trajectory of the evolution of the transcendental factor which has changed the face of the world, namely capital and the process of its accumulation, we can say that imperialism is piratry transplanted from the seas to dry land, piratry reorganised, consolidated and adapted to the aim of exploiting the natural and human resources of our peoples. But if we can calmly analyse the imperialist phenomenon, we will not shock anybody by admitting that imperialism— and everything goes to prove that it is in fact the last phase in the evolution of capitalism—has been a historical necessity, a consequence of the impetus given by the productive forces and of the transformations of the means of production in the general context of humanity, considered as one movement, that is to say a necessity like those today of the national liberation of peoples, the destruction of capital and the advent of socialism.

The important thing for our peoples is to know whether imperialism, in its role as capital in action, has fulfilled in our countries its historical mission : the acceleration of the process of development of the productive forces and their transformation in the sense of increasing complexity in the means of production; increasing the differentiation between the classes with the development of the bourgeoisie, and intensifying the class struggle; and appreciably increasing the level of economic, social and cultural life of the peoples. It is also worth examining the influences and effects of imperialist action on the social structures and historical processes of our peoples.

We will not condemn nor justify imperialism here; we will simply state that as much on the economic level as on the social and cultural level, imperialist capital has not remotely fulfilled the historical mission carried out by capital in the countries of accumulation. This means that if, on the one hand, imperialist capital has had, in the great majority of the dominated countries, the simple function of multiplying surplus value, it can be seen on the other hand that the historical capacity of capital (as indestructible accelerator of the process of development of productive forces) depends strictly on its freedom, that is to say on the degree of independence with which it is utilized. We must however recognise that in certain cases imperialist capital or moribund capitalism has had sufficient self-interest, strength and time to increase the level of productive forces (as well as building towns) and to allow a minority of the local population to attain a higher and even privileged standard of living, thus contributing to a process which some would call dialectical, by widening the contradictions within the societies in question. In other, even rarer cases, there has existed the possibility of accumulation of capital, creating the conditions for the development of a local bourgeoisie.

On the question of the effects of imperialist domination on the social structure and historical process of our peoples, we should first of all examine the general forms of imperialist domination. There are at least two forms: the first is direct domination, by means of a political power made up of people foreign to the dominated people (armed forces, police, administrative agents and settlers); this is generally called *classical colonialism or colonialism*. The second form is indirect domination, by a political power made up mainly or completely of native agents; this is called *neocolonialism*.

In the first case, the social structure of the dominated people, whatever its stage of development, can suffer the following consequences: (a) total destruction, generally accompanied by immediate or gradual elimination of the native population and, consequently, by the substitution of a population from outside; (b) partial destruction, generally accompanied by a greater or lesser influx of population from outside; (c) apparent conservation, conditioned by confining the native society to zones or reserves generally offering no possibilities of living, accompanied by massive implantation of population from outside.

The two latter cases are those which we must consider in the framework of the problematic national liberation, and they are extensively present in Africa. One can say that in either case the influence of imperialism on the historical process of the dominated people produces paralysis, stagnation and even in some cases regression in this process. However this paralysis is not complete. In one sector or another of the socio-economic whole in question, noticeable trans-formations can be expected, caused by the permanent action of some internal (local) factors or by the action of new factors introduced by the colonial domination, such as the introduction of money and the development of urban centres. Among these transformations we should particularly note, in certain cases, the progressive loss of prestige of the ruling native classes or sectors, the forced or voluntary exodus of part of the peasant population to the urban centres, with the consequent development of new social strata; salaried workers, clerks, employees in commerce and the liberal professions, and an instable stratum of unemployed. In the countryside there develops, with very varied intensity and always linked to the urban milieu, a stratum made up of small landowners. In the case of neo-colonialism, whether the majority of the colonised population is of native or foreign origin, the imperialist action takes the form of creating a local bourgeoisie or pseudo-bourgeoisie, controlled by the ruling class of the dominating country.

The transformations in the social structure are not so marked in the lower strata, above all in the countryside, which retains the characteristics of the colonial phase; but the creation of a native pseudo-bourgeoisie which generally develops out of a petty bourgeoisie of bureaucrats and accentuates the differentiation between the social strata and intermediaries in the commercial system (compradores), by strengthening the economic activity of local elements, opens up new perspectives in the social dynamic, mainly by the development of an urban working class, the introduction of private agricultural property and the progressive appearance of an agricultural proletariat. These more or less noticeable transformations of the social structure, produced by a significant increase in the level of productive forces, have a direct influence on the historical process of the socio-economic whole in question. While in classical colonialism this process is paralysed, neo-colonialist domination, by allowing the social dynamic to awaken (conflicts of interests between native social strata or class struggles), creates the illusion that the historical process is returning to its normal evolution. This illusion will be reinforced by the existence of a political power (national state) composed of native elements. In reality it is scarcely even an illusion, since the submission of the local 'ruling' class to the ruling class of the dominating country limits or prevents the development of the national productive forces. But in the concrete conditions of the present-day world economy this dependence is fatal and thus the local pseudo-bourgeoisie, however strongly nationalist it may be, cannot effectively fulfil its historical function; it cannot *freely* direct the development of the productive forces; in brief it cannot be a national bourgeoisie. For as we have seen, the productive forces are the motive force of history, and total freedom of the process of their development is an indispensable condition for their proper functioning.

We therefore see that both in colonialism and in neo-colonialism the essential characteristic of imperialist domination remains the same: the negation of the historical process of the dominated people by means of violent usurpation of the freedom of development of the national productive forces. This observation, which identifies the essence of the two apparent forms of imperialist domination, seems to us to be of major importance for the thought and action of liberation movements, both in the course of struggle and after the winning of independence.

On the basis of this, we can state that national liberation is the phenomenon in which a given socio-economic whole rejects the negation of its historical process. In other words, the national liberation of a people is the regaining of the historical personality of that people, its return to history through the destruction of the imperialist domination to which it was subjected.

We have seen that violent usurpation of the freedom of the process of development of the productive forces of the dominated socio-economic whole constitutes the principal and permanent characteristic of imperialist domination, whatever its form. We have also seen that this freedom alone can guarantee the normal development of the historical process of a people. We can therefore conclude that national liberation exists only when the national productive forces have been completely freed from every kind of foreign domination.

It is often said that national liberation is based on the right of every people to freely control its own destiny and that the objective of this liberation is national independence. Although we do not disagree with this vague and subjective way of expressing a complex reality, we prefer to be objective, since for us the basis of national liberation, whatever the formulas adopted on the level of international law, is the inalienable right of every people to have its own history, and the objective of national liberation is to regain this right usurped by imperialism, that is to say, to free the process of development of the national productive forces.

For this reason, in our opinion, any national liberation movement which does not take into consideration this basis and this objective may certainly struggle against imperialism, but will surely not be struggling for national liberation.

This means that, bearing in mind the essential characteristics of the present world economy, as well as experiences already gained in the field of anti-imperialist struggle, the principal aspect of national liberation struggle is the struggle against neo-colonialism. Furthermore, if we accept that national liberation demands a profound mutation in the process of development of the productive forces, we see that this phenomenon of *national liberation* necessarily corresponds to a *revolution*. The important thing is to be conscious of the objective and subjective conditions in which this revolution can be made and to know the type or types of struggle most appropriate for its realisation.

We are not going to repeat here that these conditions are

favourable in the present phase of the history of humanity; it is sufficient to recall that unfavourable conditions also exist, just as much on the international level as on the internal level of each nation struggling for liberation.

On the international level, it seems to us that the following factors, at least, are unfavourable to national liberation movements: the neo-colonial situation of a great number of states which, having won political independence, are now tending to join up with others already in that situation; the progress made by neo-capitalism, particularly in Europe, where imperialism is adopting preferential investments, encouraging the development of a privileged proletariat and thus lowering the revolutionary level of the working classes; the open or concealed neo-colonial position of some European states which, like Portugal, still have colonies; the so-called policy of 'aid for undeveloped countries' adopted by imperialism with the aim of creating or reinforcing native pseudo-bourgeoisies which are necessarily dependent on the international bourgeoisie, and thus obstructing the path of revolution; the claustrophobia and revolutionary timidity which have led some recently independent states whose internal economic and political conditions are favourable to revolution to accept compromises with the enemy or its agents; the growing contradictions between anti-imperialist states; and, finally, the threat to world peace posed by the prospect of atomic war on the part of imperialism. All these factors reinforce the action of imperialism against the national liberation movements.

If the repeated interventions and growing aggressiveness of imperialism against the peoples can be interpreted as a sign of desperation faced with the size of the national liberation movements, they can also be explained to a certain extent by the weaknesses produced by these unfavourable factors within the general front of the anti-imperialist struggle.

On the internal level, we believe that the most important weaknesses or unfavourable factors are inherent in the socio-economic structure and in the tendencies of its evolution under imperialist pressure, or to be more precise in the little or no attention paid to the characteristics of this structure and these tendencies by the national liberation movements in deciding on the strategy of their struggles.

By saying this we do not wish to diminish the importance of other internal factors which are unfavourable to national liberation, such as economic under-development, the consequent social and cultural backwardness of the popular masses, tribalism and other contradictions of lesser importance. It should however be pointed out that the existence of tribes only manifests itself as an important contradiction as a function of opportunistic attitudes, generally on the part of detribalised individuals or groups, within the national liberation movements. Contradictions between classes, even when only embryonic, are of far greater importance than contradictions between tribes.

Although the colonial and neo-colonial situations are identical in essence, and the main aspect of the struggle against imperialism is neo-colonialist, we feel it is vital to distinguish in practice these two situations. In fact the horizontal structure, however it may differ from the native society, and the absence of a political power composed of national elements in the colonial situation make possible the creation of a wide front of unity and struggle, which is vital to the success of the national liberation movement. But this possibility does not remove the need for a rigorous analysis of the native social structure, of the tendencies of its evolution, and for the adoption in practice of appropriate measures for ensuring true national liberation. While recognising that each movement knows best what do do in its own case, one of these measures seems to us indispensable, namely the creation of a firmly united vanguard, conscious of the true meaning and objective of the national liberation struggle which it must lead. This necessity is all the more urgent since we know that with rare exceptions the colonial situation neither permits nor needs the existence of significant vanguard classes (working class conscious of its existence and rural proletariat) which could ensure the vigilance of the popular masses over the evolution of the liberation movement. On the contrary, the generally embryonic character of the working classes and the economic, social and cultural situation of the physical force of most importance in the national liberation struggle —the peasantry—do not allow these two main forces to distinguish true national independence from fictitious political independence. Only a revolutionary vanguard, generally an active minority, can be aware of this distinction from the start and make it known, through the struggle, to the popular masses. This explains the fundamentally political nature of the national liberation struggle and to a certain extent makes the form of struggle important in the final result of the phenomenon of national liberation.

In the neo-colonial situation the more or less vertical structure of the native society and the existence of a political power composed of native elements—national state —already worsen the contradictions within that society and make difficult if not impossible the creation of as wide a front as in the colonial situation. On the one hand the material effects (mainly the nationalisation of cadres and the increased economic initiative of the native elements, particularly in the commercial field) and the psychological effects (pride in the belief of being ruled by one's own compatriots, exploitation of religious or tribal solidarity between some leaders and a fraction of the masses) together demobilise a considerable part of the nationalist forces. But on the other hand the necessarily repressive nature of the neo-colonial state against the national liberation forces, the sharpening of contradictions between classes, the objective permanence of signs and agents of foreign domination (settlers who retain their privileges, armed forces, racial discrimination), the growing poverty of the peasantry and the more or less notorious influence of external factors all contribute towards keeping the flame of nationalism alive, towards progressively raising the consciousness of wide popular sectors and towards reuniting the majority of the population, on the very basis of awareness of neo-colonialist frustration, around the ideal of national liberation. In addition, while the native ruling class becomes progressively more bourgeois, the development of a working class composed of urban workers and agricultural proletarians, all exploited by the indirect domination of imperialism, opens up new perspectives for the evolution of national liberation. This working class, whatever the level of its political consciousness (given a certain minimum, namely *the awareness of its own needs),* seems to constitute the true popular vanguard of the national liberation struggle in the neo-colonial case. However it will not be able to completely fulfil its mission in this struggle (which does not end with the gaining of independence) unless it firmly unites with the other exploited strata, the peasants in general (hired men, sharecroppers, tenants and small farmers) and the nationalist petty bourgeoisie. The creation of this alliance demands the mobilisation and organisation of the nationalist forces within the framework (or by the action) of a strong and well-structured political organisation.

Another important distinction between the colonial and neo-colonial situations is in the prospects for the struggle. The colonial situation (in which the *nation class* fights the repressive forces of the bourgeoisie of the colonising country) can lead, apparently at least, to a nationalist solution (national revolution); the nation gains its independence and theoretically adopts the economic structure which best suits it. The neo-colonial situation (in which the working classes and their allies struggle simultaneously against the imperialist bourgeoisie and the native ruling class) is not resolved by a nationalist solution; it demands the destruction of the capitalist structure implanted in the national territory by imperialism, and correctly postulates a socialist solution.

This distinction arises mainly from the different levels of the productive forces in the two cases and the consequent sharpening of the class struggle.

It would not be difficult to show that in time the distinction becomes scarcely apparent. It is sufficient to recall that in our present historical situation—elimination of imperialism which uses every means to perpetuate its domination over our peoples, and consolidation of socialism throughout a large part of the world—there are only two possible paths for an independent nation: to return to imperialist domination (neo-colonialism, capitalism, state capitalism), or to take the way of socialism. This operation, on which depends the compensation for the efforts and sacrifices of the popular masses during the struggle, is considerably influenced by the form of struggle and the degree of revolutionary consciousness of those who lead it. The facts make it unnecessary for us to prove that the essential instrument of imperialist domination is violence. If we accept the principle that the *liberation struggle is a revolution* and that it does not finish at the moment when the national flag is raised and the national anthem played, we will see that there is not, and cannot be national liberation without the use of liberating violence by the nationalist forces, to answer the criminal violence of the agents of imperialism. Nobody can doubt that, whatever its local characteristics, imperialist domination implies a state of permanent violence against the nationalist forces. There is no people on earth which, having been subjected to the imperialist yoke (colonialist or neo-colonialist), has managed to gain its independence (nominal or effective) without victims. The important thing is to determine which forms of violence have to be used by the national liberation forces in order not only to answer the violence of imperialism but also to ensure through the struggle the final victory of their cause, true national indipendence. The past and present experiences of various peoples, the present situation of national liberation struggles in the world (especially in Vietnam, the Congo and Zimbabwe) as well as the situation of permanent violence, or at least of contradictions and upheavals, in certain countries which have gained their independence by the so-called peaceful way, show us not only that compromises with imperialism do not work, but also that the normal way of national liberation, imposed on peoples by imperialist repression, is *armed struggle*.

We do not think we will shock this assembly by stating that the only effective way of definitively fulfilling the aspirations of the peoples, that is to say of attaining national liberation, is by armed struggle. This is the great lesson which the contemporary history of liberation struggle teaches all those who are truly committed to the effort of liberating their peoples.

It is obvious that both the effectiveness of this way and the stability of the situation to which it leads after liberation depend not only on the characteristics of the organisation of the struggle but also on the political and moral awareness of those who, for historical reasons, are capable of being the immediate heirs of the colonial or neo-colonial state. For events have shown that the only social sector capable of being aware of the reality of imperialist domination and of directing the state apparatus inherited from this domination is the native petty bourgeoisie. If we bear in mind the aleatory characteristics and the complexity of the tendencies naturally inherent in the economic situation of this social stratum or class, we will see that this specific inevitability in our situation constitutes one of the weaknesses of the national liberation movement.

The colonial situation, which does not permit the development of a native pseudo-bourgeoisie and in which the popular masses do not generally reach the necessary level of political consciousness before the advent of the phenomenon of national liberation, offers the petty bourgeoisie the historical opportunity of leading the struggle against foreign domination, since by nature of its objective and subjective position (higher standard of living than that of the masses, more frequent contact with the agents of colonialism, and hence more chances of being humiliated, higher level of education and political awareness, etc.) it is the stratum which most rapidly becomes aware of the need to free itself from foreign domination. This historical responsibility is assumed by the sector of the petty bourgeoisie which, in the colonial context, can be called *revolutionary,* while other sectors retain the doubts characteristic of these classes or ally themselves to colonialism so as to defend, albeit illusorily, their social situation.

The neo-colonial situation, which demands the elimination of the native pseudo-bourgeoisie so that national liberation can be attained, also offers the petty bourgeoisie the chance of playing a role of major and even decisive importance in the struggle for the elimination of foreign domination. But in this case, by virtue of the progress made in the social structure, the function of leading the struggle is shared (to a greater or lesser extent) with the more educated sectors of the working classes and even with some elements of the national pseudo-bourgeoisie who are inspired by patriotic sentiments. The role of the sector of the petty bourgeoisie which participates in leading the struggle is all the more important since it is a fact that in the neo-colonial situation it is the most suitable sector to assume these functions, both because of the economic and cultural limitations of the working masses, and because of the complexes and limitations of an ideological nature which characterise the sector of the national pseudo-bourgeoisie which supports the struggle. In this case it is important to note that the role with which it is entrusted demands from this sector of the petty bourgeoisie a greater revolutionary consciousness, and the capacity for faithfully interpreting the aspirations of the masses in each phase of the struggle and for identifying themselves more and more with the masses.

But however high the degree of revolutionary consciousness of the sector of the petty bourgeoisie called on to fulfil this historical function, it cannot free itself from one objective reality: the petty bourgeoisie, as a service class (that is to say that a class not directly involved in the process of production) does not possess the economic base to guarantee the taking over of power. In fact history has shown that whatever the role—sometimes important—played by individuals coming from the petty bourgeoisie in the process of a revolution, this class has never possessed political control. And it could never possess it, since political control (the state) is based on the economic capacity of the ruling class, and in the conditions of colonial and neo-colonial society this capacity is retained by two entities: imperialist capital and the native working classes.

To retain the power which national liberation puts in its hands, the petty bourgeoisie has only one path: to give free rein to its natural tendencies to become more bourgeois, to permit the development of a bureaucratic and intermediary bourgeoisie in the commercial cycle, in order to transform itself into a national pseudo-bourgeoisie, that is to say in order to negate the revolution and necessarily ally itself with imperialist capital. Now all this corresponds to the neo-colonial situation, that is, to the betrayal of the objectives of national liberation. In order not to betray these objectives, the petty bourgeoisie has only one choice: to strengthen its revolutionary consciousness, to reject the temptations of becoming more bourgeois and the natural concerns of its class mentality, to identify itself with the working classes and not to oppose the normal development of the process of revolution. This means that in order to truly fulfil the role in the national liberation struggle, the revolutionary petty bourgeoisie must be capable of committing suicide as a class in order to be reborn as revolutionary workers, completely identified with the deepest aspirations of the people to which they belong.

This alternative—to betray the revolution or to commit suicide as a class—constitutes the dilemma of the petty bourgeoisie in the general framework of the national liberation struggle. The positive solution in favour of the revolution depends on what Fidel Castro recently correctly called *the development of revolutionary consciousness*. This dependence necessarily calls our attention to the capacity of the leader of the national liberation struggle to remain faithful to the principles and to the fundamental cause of this struggle. This shows us, to a certain extent, that if national liberation is essentially a political problem, the conditions for its development give it certain characteristics which belong to the sphere of morals.

We will not shout hurrahs or proclaim here our solidarity with this or that people in struggle. Our presence is in itself a cry of condemnation of imperialism and a proof of solidarity with all peoples who want to banish from their country the imperialist yoke, and in particular with the heroic people of Vietnam. But we firmly believe that the best proof we can give of our anti-imperialist position and of our active solidarity with our comrades in this common struggle is to return to our countries, to further develop this struggle and to remain faithful to the principles and objectives of national liberation.

Our wish is that every national liberation movement represented here may be able to repeat in its own country, arms in hand, in unison with its people, the already legendary cry of Cuba:
PATRIA O MUERTE, VENCEREMOS!
DEATH TO THE FORCES OF IMPERIALISM!
FREE, PROSPEROUS AND HAPPY COUNTRY FOR EACH OF OUR PEOPLES!
VENCEREMOS!

The development of the struggle

*Extracts from a declaration made to the OSPAAAL
General Secretariat in December 1968*

1. Synthesis of the situation

The main characteristic of the present phase of our
liberation struggle is the progressive reversal of the relative
positions of the two forces. While the Portuguese colonialist
forces are falling back more and more on the defensive, our
patriotic forces are developing the offensive both against the
fortified enemy camps still remaining in the liberated areas
and against the colonial troops in the other regions. While
our action is increasingly assuming the character of a mobile
partisan war and we are reinforcing the capacity of co-
ordination of our activities on the different fronts, the
enemy's actions are becoming infrequent, being mainly
restricted to acts of reprisal, terrorism and plunder, with
increasingly frequent aerial bombing and machine-gunning.
Meanwhile, having succeeded in consolidating the areas
liberated and controlled by our armed forces under the
auspices of the Party's governing bodies, we are making
fruitful efforts there towards improving the production of
foodstuffs, education and health facilities—developing the
new bases of our political, economic, administrative,
judicial, social and cultural life.

Apart from in the Cabo Verde and Bissagos Islands, and in
the main urban areas (Bissao, Bafata and Gabo-Sara), where
our action is still restricted to a purely political level, the
enemy is having to face the initiatives of our armed forces
on every side.

Also, having succeeded in constantly frustrating the political
manoeuvres of the Portuguese colonialists, aimed at creating
divisions within the patriotic forces and mystifying national
and international opinion, our armed and political actions
have put a halt to the collaborationist activities of certain
traditional chiefs who were traitors to the nation, thus
neutralising the harmful effects of their attitude on certain
sections of the population.

In the contested or partially liberated areas, we are
constantly broadening the fronts of our struggle and, in the
flame of patriotism fanned by the fire of our weapons,
nursing the future of freedom, peace and progress for which
we are fighting.

The Portuguese information services themselves have had
to admit, through the voice of Radio Bissao, that "the

bandits no longer want to stay in the bush; they are moving into the villages and drawing closer to the urban centres." This reality is proudly expressed in one of our people's patriotic songs, which runs: "Lala kêmà: kàu di sukundi kâ tê" (The great humid plain has caught fire: they [the colonialists] have nowhere to hide).

2. Situation of the armed struggle

The colonialist forces now number about 25 thousand men (army, navy and air force, police and special armed corps), with the reinforcements newly arrived from Lisbon, especially since last May, to counterbalance the intensification of our action and to replace the heavy losses suffered during the course of this year. For a small underdeveloped country such as ours (15,500 square miles, 800,000 inhabitants, of whom only about 100,000 are capable of usefully assisting our action against the enemy) an army of 25,000 well-equipped men, with the most modern material resources, assumes astronomic proportions, comparable only to those of the disaster which they are doomed to face in our country. And this in spite of huge expenditure on material of all sorts, and particularly American B26 bombers and German jet fighters (Fiat 91).

Portuguese actions, the frequency of which has dropped significantly in recent months, are characterised mainly by:
a) aerial bombing and intensive machine-gunning of the villages in the liberated areas and of places believed to conceal our bases;
b) a few vain attempts to land troops and set up camps in our liberated areas (particularly in the South of the country) with massive air support;
c) increasingly rare incursions into certain liberated areas close to the fortified camps, with the aim of terrorising the population, ruining the villages and destroying our crops and cattle;
d) desperate attempts to bring supplies into certain fortified camps by river and by air, rarely by land;
e) a few larger-scale operations in contested areas.

The bombing and machine-gunning of villages and of our positions by their planes is the main action at present carried out by the enemy, this being in certain areas, and for long periods, the only manifestation of their presence. Several villages have been destroyed in recent months, notably in the North and Central-South of the country. This is understandable if one bears in mind the weakness of our means of anti-aircraft defence and our forces' lack of experience in this field. The civil defence measures which we have nevertheless taken have successfully prevented extensive loss of life among our peoples, frustrating the genocidal intentions of the Portuguese colonialists.

Attempts to land troops in our liberated areas with the aim of creating bridgeheads there have ended in failure. Except in very rare cases (using helicopter-borne troops) when the enemy has been able to destroy crops and cattle, their terrorist operations have generally ended in considerable losses for them in lives and material. Getting supplies to the fortified camps which are completely cut off by us is one of the major problems facing the enemy. With the support of aircraft which bomb and strafe the river banks, the enemy does still manage to supply certain camps by river.

In the contested areas, joint operations (called 'mopping-up operations') are generally just a waste of energy, as our forces take advantage of these opportunities to wreak havoc on the men and equipment of the enemy forces in ambushes and surprise attacks. This is proved by the fact that in spite of the numerous operations of this type carried out in the regions of Canchungo, S. Domingos and Bafata, we have made considerable progress there, liberating new areas and controlling certain roads.

The adoption of the technique of strategic hamlets has not produced the expected results. Created mainly in areas under the influence of certain traditional chiefs, particularly in Gabu, these hamlets have been subjected to violent attacks by our troops and several of them have been destroyed. The populations, more realistic than the chiefs, are now fleeing from the hamlets, preferring to take refuge in neighbouring countries, or moving into the liberated areas or the urban centres. In addition, information from colonialist sources indicates that the morale of the Portuguese troops is getting progressively lower. Conflicts inside the barracks and the fortified camps are becoming more frequent. After the attempted armed rebellion within the air force in April 1965, which led to the arrest of over 100 military, including a senior officer sentenced to 28 years in prison, several other conflicts, generally severely repressed, have taken place in the course of the past year.

More than 7,000 young men, drafted into the army and destined mainly for our country, have been able to desert and hide in the countryside, or get abroad, especially to France.

Our own actions have been characterised mainly by the following activities:
a) attacks on barracks and fortified camps, particularly on those remaining in our liberated areas. These attacks have been made with mortars, artillery and bazookas. In the case of the weaker camps they have been followed by assaults using light weapons;
b) increasing the isolation of enemy positions by using heavy

weapons against river transports, and by installing anti-aircraft weapons; destruction of the strategic hamlets;

c) ambushes and surprise attacks against enemy forces moving in contested or partially liberated areas; control of the main roads in these areas;

d) raids against the barracks in the areas that have not yet been liberated, aimed at increasing the insecurity of the enemy forces and of the individuals supporting them;

e) active defence and reinforcement of vigilance in our liberated areas.

The increasing use of aircraft and helicopters reflects the difficulties experienced by the colonial authorities in supplying their troops. In fact, given the impossibility of using almost all passable roads, including those in contested areas, and faced with the intensification of our action against river transports, the enemy is forced to use air transport to keep the troops supplied. Although we have sunk or seriously damaged several boats on the Farim, Cumbidjà and Geba rivers, our action in this field, as in the field of anti-aircraft defence (3 planes shot down and several others damaged) still shows serious deficiencies, particularly in cases where the river transports are escorted by aircraft.

Increasing the isolation of the enemy forces, which also demands the urgent development of effective anti-aircraft measures, is proving to be an indispensable measure for accelerating the total defeat of these forces. This isolation leads to physical and moral degeneration among the troops, and facilitates our actions against the fortified camps.

It is in ambushes and surprise attacks carried out mainly in the contested areas that we are inflicting the heaviest loss of life and destruction of equipment on the enemy forces. In fact, as the colonialist troops venture only very rarely into our liberated areas, it is elsewhere that we are really able to fully develop our military action, in the field of guerilla warfare. We can now state firmly that any attempt by the enemy to reoccupy the liberated areas will end in defeat, or will cost them an even higher price, in lives and equipment, than they paid at the time of the invasion of the island of Como in 1964.

We have made progress in co-ordinating the actions of our armed forces within each sector, and we are trying to effectively co-ordinate our forces on the regional and national level.

In the Cabo Verde Islands our Party, which has consolidated its bases and made major progress in mobilising the popular masses, has decided to move on to armed action as soon as possible, in order to answer the criminal violence of the colonialist agents. Despite the difficulties inherent in this, we must develop the struggle by every possible means in this part of our territory, and we will do so.

The situation on the level of the armed struggle is therefore generally favourable. The enemy is on the defensive, and we hold the initiative on all fronts. We must not lose sight of the fact, however, that the enemy, economically much stronger than us, has considerable human resources and efficient material means available with which to continue the war against us. They are still firmly established in certain urban areas, particularly in the main towns, and can still count on the money, arms, aircraft and other equipment which their allies are supplying.

3. The political situation

The political conditions in our country before the beginning of our struggle—nationwide oppression, absence of even the most elementary freedoms, police and military repression —determined our actions, forcing us to start the armed liberation struggle. Now it is the latter—as the expression of our determination to free ourselves from the colonial yoke, and thus of our fundamental political choice—which is determining the enemy's political behaviour.

Swept out for good from our liberated areas, which cover more than half our national territory (about 60%) and in which 50% of our people live, Portuguese 'sovereignty' is now limited to the urban areas. In fact Portuguese political domination, which generally took the form of more or less forced collection of taxes of every sort, has ceased to be possible even in the contested or partially liberated areas. In general the inhabitants of these areas refuse to pay taxes. The colonial authorities have to tolerate this refusal, fearing that the use of force would produce a mass exodus of the inhabitants towards the liberated areas or neighbouring countries. Even in the urban centres, including the main towns, effective political control has become practically impossible, in the face of the growing influx of refugees from the combat zones and of the pressure maintained on these centres by our armed forces.

Having counted on the treachery of certain traditional chiefs who had promised the loyalty of the populations under their control, the Portuguese authorities now have to recognise their failure on this level, and have even stripped of their rank or arrested some of these chiefs. Progressively abandoned by the populations which they had controlled, the traditional chiefs who have betrayed their nation are today the object of suspicion from the colonial authorities and cannot hide their fear and their doubts when faced with the progress of our struggle.

The political manoeuvres of the Portuguese colonialists

aimed at demobilising patriots and deceiving African and world opinion by promulgating false administrative 'reforms' and hinting at so-called internal autonomy, distant and undefined, have also met with failure.

A large part of the sector of the African petty bourgeoisie which had placed itself at the service of the colonialists, now has to face an agonising situation, prey to a double fear— that of the colonialist-fascist repression, and that of the justice of the patriotic forces. Some of these petty-bourgeois elements have been moved, or have asked to be moved (to Angola, Mozambique or Portugal), others have been arrested, and the majority hope to be able to go on deceiving the colonial authorities and managing to convince us of their nationalist feelings.

The dominant factor in the political sphere is the backlash of police repression, which is now striking not only patriots but also people who were considered favourable to the colonial regime. The President of our Party, Rafael Barbosa (Zaim Lopez) who was living under house arrest, has again been secretly moved to Bissao prison. The patriots Fernando Fortes, Quintino Nosolini and others, who had already suffered three years' imprisonment, have been imprisoned again. The concentration camp on the island of Galinhas is being filled with patriots suspected of being members or sympathisers of our Party. About 80 patriots, among them some Party cadres, are still being detained in inhuman conditions in the infamous concentration camp of Tarrafal (Cabo Verde Islands). In addition certain people in the service of Portuguese colonialism have been arrested, and others, including Duarte Vieira and Godofredo de Souza, have died under interrogation. The lawyer Augusto Silva and the important businessman Severino de Pina, General Secretary of the Municipality of Bissao, have been arrested and transferred to the prison of Caxias, near Lisbon. These recent events demonstrate the confusion of the colonial authorities, under the local direction of 'governor' Arnaldo Schultz, trained by the Nazis and formerly Salazar's Minister of the Interior.

The main characteristics of our political action are the work of consolidating our national organisation and adapting its structure and its leadership to the new demands of the struggle. In the liberated areas we have strengthened the leadership organisation of the Party (inter-regional committee) by permanently establishing two members of the Political Bureau in each inter-region. The sector committees are developing their action among the population and a large number of village committees (section committees) have been created or renewed. The Party is making efforts to guarantee the normal and effective functioning of the base organisations, in the framework of a wide democracy under centralised leadership. In the contested or partially liberated areas political work is carried out mainly by the armed forces.

In the urban centres, in spite of the police and military repression, our militants are continuing to develop their underground work and maintain contact with the leadership. Our organisation has been consolidated in Bissao, Bolama and Bafata, the main towns.

The higher Party organs are functioning normally and are dedicating themselves to the improvement of political work at all levels and to solving the various problems posed by the rapid development of our struggle. There have been four conferences of cadres this year, two for each inter-region. The work of these conferences, which have concentrated on the problems of organisation of the struggle and development of the liberated areas (production, security, education and health), has constituted a basis for elaborating general and specific directives for leaders at all levels. These conferences of cadres also gave attention to the study of the deficiencies and mistakes committed in our political and armed actions. Measures have been taken to progressively eliminate deficiencies and rule out mistakes.

4. Economic situation

For some time now we have been able to eliminate the system of colonialist exploitation of our people in most of the national territory. This year we struck a severe blow against the remains of the economy of exploitation in the Eastern (Gabu-Bafata) and Western (Canchungo-S.Domingos) regions.

Most wholesale and retail businesses in the secondary urban centres have had to close down, as the merchants and employees have fled from these centres to the capital. To get some idea of the catastrophic situation of the colonial economy, it is enough to recall that the Companhia Uniao Fabril (CUF), the main commercial enterprise in Guinea, has been in deficit for almost three years, and has had to draw on its reserves to survive. In addition the colonial authorities, in a country which produces more rice than is needed for local consumption, have had to import large quantities of this cereal (10,000 tons from Brazil alone) to feed the troops and the urban populations.

Other economic activities have been practically paralysed. Apart from works of a military nature, public works and building are non-existent.

In the liberated areas we are continuing to give every attention to economic development, particularly with regard to increasing the production of crops. New areas of land were planted with rice and other crops during the last rainy season. Other products (leather, rubber from the forests, crocodile and other animal skins, and coconuts) have been shipped and sold abroad, although only in small quantities.

We are also trying to develop artisan work and small local industries. Because of technical difficulties (lack of means of transport and spare parts) we have had to postpone the reopening of the sawmills previously belonging to settlers in the forest of Dio. We are currently examining the possibility of starting up in the North a small rudimentary factory to produce ordinary soap, using palm oil.

To supply the basic needs of the population, two new people's stores have been created in the North of the country and in the Boe region. However we are facing grave difficulties in this, through lack of merchandise, in spite of the help given by friendly countries. Supplying the basic necessities of the inhabitants of the liberated areas is proving to be a major factor in the consolidation of these areas, giving encouragement in the struggle and demoralising the enemy.

The colonialists are making efforts to compete with our people's stores by greatly reducing the prices of goods in the areas which have not yet been liberated. We must successfully counter this competition. Every effort and sacrifice made with this aim will have favourable repercussions on the evolution of the struggle.

5. Social and cultural situation

In order to counter the success of our struggle, the enemy has made efforts to improve certain social conditions, particularly in the urban centres, and even has extensive propaganda, mainly on the radio, aimed at convincing the population that it should repudiate our Party, claiming that life will be a 'bed of roses' if the 'Portuguese presence' is maintained in our country.

The flooding of thousands of people towards the main towns has created serious problems of overpopulation there, with effects on food supplies and on common crime. Unemployment is constantly growing. The hospitals and even the schools are occupied by troops, because of the lack of military installations. In Bissao, where the population has trebled in the last two years, theft, prostitution and general moral degeneracy are rife. Even within the ranks of the colonial troops increased medical facilities have not succeeded in improving the situation, with a large proportion of the military suffering from malaria or intestinal illnesses.

In the field of education the situation is also very bad, in spite of the measures hastily taken by the colonial authorities to increase the number of official schools (from 11 to 25) and to give grants for study in Portugal. Almost all the elementary schools of the Catholic missions ceased to function years ago, when the majority of the African teachers joined our ranks. The few schools established in the unliberated areas have not even started functioning for lack of teachers, and a large proportion of the pupils have preferred to come to the nearby liberated areas and attend our schools instead. Secondary education (1 high school and 1 technical school in Bissao) uses teachers without any professional qualifications, notably the wives of officers in the colonial army and other people without any university education.

It would be naive to pretend that the progress achieved in our liberated areas has brought about a radical change in the social situation of the inhabitants. Our people, who have to face a colonial war whose genocidal intentions spare nobody, still live under difficult conditions. Entire populations have seen their villages destroyed and have had to take refuge in the bush. But everybody has enough to eat, nobody is subject to exploitation, and the standard of living is progressively rising. Demonstrating a political consciousness which is heightened every day, the people live and work in harmony, united in standing up to the evils of the war imposed on us. Apart from a few rare cases of lack of discipline, generally motivated by personal interests or understandable misconceptions, the people proudly follow the Party's directives. Four hospitals are now functioning in the interior of the country (2 in the South, 1 in the North and 1 in Boe), with a total of about 200 beds, and the permanent attendance of doctors helped by sufficient nurses and having the equipment necessary for surgical operations. Also dozens of dispensaries established in the various sectors give daily assistance to the combatants and to the people. The hospital at Boe has now been improved and has departments of general medicine, surgery, orthopaedics, radiology, anaesthesia and analysis. In the past year 80 nurses have been trained (30 inside the country and 50 in Europe), and 30 more are being trained at the moment. We are soon going to set up a new rural hospital, exclusively for orthopaedics.

Bearing in mind that we started from nothing, and that the Portuguese colonialists had only three hospitals and a few dispensaries in the whole country, the importance of the results already obtained, with the help of certain friendly countries and organisations, is obvious.

Progress made in the field of education has far surpassed what we thought possible in our conditions. 127 primary schools are now functioning in the liberated areas, attended in 1965/1966 by 13,500 pupils aged 7 to 15. Considering that at the start of our struggle there were in the whole country only 56 primary and elementary schools (11 official and 45 mission schools) with a maximum total of 2,000 pupils, it is easy to understand the enthusiasm of our children and people for the Party's success in this field.

As in other fields, progress in the field of education has brought with it new demands, and here too we are facing difficulties at present. Particular difficulties are those of publishing books in Portuguese for the various classes, of providing educational materials and clothing for the pupils, and of maintaining the pilot school and a few others set up near the frontiers. But the several thousand adults who have already learned to read and write, as well as the young people from the primary schools, are now discovering a new world before them; they understand the reasons for our struggle and our Party's aims better, and make no secret of their enthusiasm and renewed confidence in the future.

7. Our struggle in the international context

Our enemy, the Portuguese colonial government, has suffered shameful defeats on an international level this year. It has been excluded from various international organisations, including certain specialised UN agencies, and has been severely criticised and condemned within other organisations.

Although we greatly appreciate the efforts made by the United Nations and the moral and political value of its resolutions, we have no illusions about their practical effects. In fact we are convinced that given the contradictions which dominate the internal life of that international organisation and its proven inability to resolve the conflicts between colonial peoples and the dominating powers, the United Nations has done everything it can against Portuguese colonialism.

The Portuguese government is isolated internationally (as is proved by the voting at the UN), but this isolation covers only the political and moral field. In the basic fields of economics, finance and arms, which determine and condition the real political and moral behaviour of states, the Portuguese government is able to count more than ever on the effective aid of the NATO allies and others. Anyone familiar with the relations between Portugal and its allies, namely the USA, Federal Germany and other Western powers, can see that this assistance (economic, financial and in war material) is constantly increasing, in the most diverse forms, overt and convert. By skilfully playing on the contingencies of the cold war, in particular on the strategic importance of its own geographical position and that of the Azores islands, by granting military bases to the USA and Federal Germany, by flying high the false banner of the defence of Western and Christian civilisation in Africa, and by further subjecting the natural resources of the colonies and the Portuguese economy itself to the big financial monopolies, the Portuguese government has managed to guarantee for as long as necessary the assistance which it receives from the Western powers and from its racist allies in Southern Africa.

It is our duty to stress the international character of the Portuguese colonial war against Africa and the important, and even decisive role played by the USA and Federal Germany in pursuing this war. If the Portuguese government is still holding out on the three fronts of the war which it is fighting in Africa, it is because it can count on the overt or covert support of the USA, freely use NATO weapons, buy B26 aircraft for the genocide of our people (including from 'private parties'), and obtain whenever it wishes money, jet aircraft and weapons of every sort from Federal Germany where, furthermore, certain war-wounded from the Portuguese colonial army are hospitalised and treated.

It is our armed liberation struggle which will eliminate Portuguese colonialism in Africa, and at the same time put an end to the anti-African complicity of Portugal's allies. This struggle also offers us the advantage, among others, of getting to know in a real way who are the friends and who are the enemies of our people.

Various successes obtained by our delegations at international conferences, the showing of films made in our country, both in Africa (Conakry and Dakar) and in Europe, the growing support which our organisation is finding among the anti-colonialist forces—all these mark considerable progress in our action on an international level during the past year. We also presented to the UN, at the session of the Committee on Decolonialisation held in Algiers in June, some unusual evidence of our situation— that of journalists and film-makers who have visited our country, supported by ample film and photographic documentation. However, we must continue to use every possible means of improving our action on the international level.

8. Perspectives for the struggle

The central perspective for our struggle is the development and intensification of our fight on its three fundamental levels: political action, armed action, and national reconstruction. In order to do this, we must above all:
a) constantly improve and develop political work among the popular masses and the armed forces, and preserve at all costs our national unity;
b) further strengthen organisation, discipline and democracy within our Party, continually adapt it to the evolution of

the struggle, correct mistakes and demand from leaders and militants rigorous application of the principles guiding our actions;

c) improve the organisation of the armed forces, intensify our action on all fronts and develop the co-ordination of our military activities;

d) increase the isolation of the enemy forces, subject them to decisive blows and destroy the remnants of tranquillity which they still enjoy in certain urban centres;

e) defend our liberated areas against the enemy's terrorist attacks, guarantee for our people the tranquillity which is indispensable for productive work;

f) study and find the best solutions to the economic, administrative, social and cultural problems of the liberated areas, increase industrial production, however rudimentary, and continually improve health and education facilities;

g) accelerate the training of cadres;

h) fight and eliminate tendencies towards opportunism, parasitism, arrivism and deviation of our action from the general line laid down by our Party, at the service of our people;

i) strengthen and develop our relations with the peoples, states and organisations of Africa, and tighten the fraternal links which join us with the neighbouring countries and with the peoples of the other Portuguese colonies;

j) strengthen our relations of sincere collaboration with the anti-colonialist and anti-imperialist forces, for useful co-operation in the common struggle against colonialism, imperialism and racism.

Within the framework of an armed liberation struggle, whatever the stage of its evolution, no organisation would be so imprudent as to fix in advance a date for independence. We are however convinced that we have covered most of the long road to freedom and gone through the most difficult stages. This much depends essentially on us, on the efforts and sacrifices which we are prepared to make, in the framework of a multiform and necessarily rational action, which takes into acount our own experience and that of others. The continuation, the definitive success and the length of our fight must however depend, to a certain extent, on the concrete solidarity which Africa and all the anti-colonialist forces will be able to give to our people.

On freeing captured Portuguese soldiers — I

Declaration made in Dakar, Senegal, on March 3 1968

Mr President of the Senegalese Red Cross, gentlemen of the Press, dear friends:

In the framework of our struggle for national independence, peace and progress for our people in Guinea and the Cabo Verde Islands, the freeing of Portuguese soldiers captured by our armed forces was both necessary and predictable. This humanitarian gesture, whose political significance will escape nobody, is the corollary of a fundamental principle of our party and of our struggle. We are not fighting against the Portuguese people, against Portuguese individuals or families. Without ever confusing the Portuguese people with colonialism, we have had to take up arms to wipe out from our homeland the shameful domination of Portuguese colonialism. Being thus only a further proof of fidelity to the principles of our party, this action needs no commentary.

However, bearing in mind the present circumstances, and given the fact that this is the first time that, with the fraternal help of the Senegalese Red Cross, we are making this gesture and handing over to the International Red Cross three Portuguese prisoners-of-war so that they can rejoin their families and cease risking an inglorious death in our country, we wish to make the following declaration.

At this very moment, after five years of colonial war, the Portuguese colonialists are continuing to perpetrate barbarous crimes against our people, scorning the most elementary principles of morality and of present-day international law.

Hundreds of Guinean and Cabo-Verdian patriots are suffering in the inhuman conditions of the colonial political prisons and the concentration camps of the Isle of Galinhas (Guinea) and of Tarrafal (Cabo Verde). These patriots are tortured by the PIDE and several others have been brutally assassinated.

Members of our armed forces captured by the colonial troops are generally given a summary execution. Others are tortured and forced to make declarations which the colonial authorities use in their propaganda. In their vain but nonetheless criminal attempt at genocide, the Portuguese colonialists carry out daily acts of terrorism against the peaceful inhabitants of our liberated areas, particularly against women, children and old people; they bomb and machine-gun our people, reducing our villages to ashes and destroying our crops, using bombs of every type, and in particular fragmentation bombs, napalm and white phosphor bombs.

In freeing these Portuguese prisoners-of-war who, like their colleagues still in prison, have enjoyed all the prerogatives laid down by international regulations, we once again call the attention of world opinion to the crimes perpetrated in our country by the Portuguese colonialists, which they would not be able to carry out if they did not continue to receive political and material aid from their allies.

After five years of armed struggle in particularly difficult conditions, with more experience and more effective methods of action, our armed forces are stronger than ever. On the basis of the political and military progress made in our struggle, we have just inflicted a crushing failure on the Portuguese propaganda attempt which took the form of a visit to Guinea by the President of the Portuguese Republic. Both during this lightning visit, during which he travelled only by air, and in the weeks following, we attacked almost all the bases and camps of the colonial troops, inflicting considerable losses in life and equipment. Opening a new phase of our struggle, our forces have succeeded in attacking, with remarkable success, the international airport of Bissalanca, the main Portuguese airbase situated on the Isle of Bissao 10 kilometers from the capital. Elsewhere we are developing and intensifying our actions in the contested areas.

The freeing of these Portuguese prisoners-of-war, by proving our strength and the high level reached in our struggle, reaffirms our unshakable certainty of victory.

Portuguese public opinion, particularly among the popular masses and in intellectual circles, is becoming more aware each day of the necessity of acting by every available means against the colonial war. In the very heart of the Portuguese government a realist tendency is showing itself, making its voice more widely heard and seeking adequate means of making the extremists understand that the colonial war is not only useless but irremediably lost in our country. In addition, the number of Portuguese military men who want to abandon the war is growing every day, as is confirmed by information from reliable sources and from the declarations of recent deserters.

The freeing of these three prisoners-of-war is a stimulus to the Portuguese people in its struggle against the colonial war, to the realists within the Portuguese government itself, and to those elements among the colonial troops who want to free themselves from the nightmare of a war which is against the interests of their own people.

The major aim of our struggle is to gain national independence for our people. This is why our struggle is fundamentally a political one, and as we have always stated, we are ready at any time to cease hostilities in order to find a political solution to the conflict which opposes our people to the government of Portugal. Our only condition is the unequivocal recognition by that government of our inalienable right to independence.

Some will interpret this freeing of prisoners-of-war as a token of goodwill on our part. But not the Portuguese government, which continues to claim 'the right and the duty' to defend Western and Christian civilisation on our continent, in collaboration with the racist regimes of Southern Africa and by using torture, terrorism, napalm and the most revolting crimes against the peoples of Africa.

Our humanitarian gesture, which will surely be understood by all men who love peace, freedom and progress, does not diminish in any way our determination to go on fighting until Portuguese colonialism has been totally eliminated in our country. In doing this, we are conscious of serving the interests of our people and of Africa.

The three prisoners
Jose Vieira Lauro (captured on the Southern Front on October 6 1965), Eduardo Duas Vieira (captured on the Eastern Front on December 2 1965) and Manuel Fragata Francisco (captured on the Northern Front on December 18 1967).

On freeing captured Portuguese soldiers — II

Declaration made in Dakar, Senegal, on December 19 1968

When we freed three Portuguese prisoners-of-war last March, we emphasised the normality and necessity of our gesture in the framework of the political and humanitarian principles guiding our struggle. By repeating this gesture today and freeing another three prisoners-of-war we risk falling into a routine. However this cannot alter the essentially political character of our initiative.

This action is taking place after the political death of Salazar who, unable to live out his time, carries on his moribund shoulders the chief responsibility for the crimes committed against our people, against other African peoples and against his own people. While the political death of the Portuguese dictator has not given rise to illusions among us—since our people and our combatants are aware of the fact that we are fighting Portuguese colonialism, which we have never confused with the policy of a single man—certain changes are nevertheless possible in Portuguese internal politics, particularly with regard to the style of government and repression. These changes could become accentuated in the long term, both as a result of the growing pressure of new phenomena which have arisen and will arise within Portuguese political life (which is conditioned and trauma- tised by the colonial wars) and through the need for the new President of the Council to progressively affirm his own personality. In this connection some people think that Mr Marcelo Caetano, being younger than his predecessor but more permeable to the historical realities of our times, will come to understand the irreversible character of our struggle for national liberation and the inevitability of the accession of our African people to national independence, which is the only possible outcome to the war imposed on us by Portuguese colonialism.

In his speech to the Portuguese National Assembly on November 27th, the new President of the Council gave special emphasis to the desperate situation of the colonial war in our country. In doing this he not only rendered indirect homage to our people and our Party, whose prestige was thereby increased on an international level, but also showed an acute awareness of reality. His use of Salazarist jargon and of certain patriotic mystification, and his dramatic evocation of the scarecrow of *communist subversion* do not significantly limit the importance of his speech, and can be explained by the pressing need to appease the *ultras* and to moderate the action of those Portuguese of all levels, above all young people and students, who are daring to proclaim their hostility to the colonial war. While declaring his determination to keep our people under the colonial yoke "at any price" the head of the Portuguese government knows very well that quite apart from the enormous and irrecoverable losses in Portuguese lives and equipment the worst price of all will be that of seeing our people sweep from our country every sort of Portuguese presence, which is becoming too heavily stained by the crimes of the colonial war and the attempted genocide of our people. The best price would be to be realistic, to bravely face up to the *hawks* of the colonial war and to obey the demands of history: to negotiate with our Party our people's accession to independence (since we already control more than two thirds of our national territory) and in this way to preserve the possibilities of co-operation which would be useful to both countries.

At a time when we are intensifying our struggle on all fronts, inflicting new and more crushing defeats on the colonial troops, the freeing of these three prisoners-of-war is yet another proof (if proof is needed) of our sovereignty and independence of thought and action. The Portuguese government and its allies on whom the continuation of the criminal war against our people is crucially dependent, must be aware that if we decided to fight and accept every sort of sacrifice for the independence of our country—of which we are the leaders and legitimate representatives—it was certainly not in order to hand over our country and islands to other foreign powers.

It being only a few days to the great universal festival of the family, some will see in our gesture an act of Christian charity. Those same people, together with history, should conclude that our people, made up of animists, Islamised and Christian peoples, has no need of the Portuguese colonial presence in order to prove its civilisation and awareness of its responsibilities.

These young Portuguese being returned to their families at this year's end, when humanity is still anxiously wondering about the imperialist threats to peace and international security, are witnesses to our confidence in the future and bearers of our wishes for freedom for the people of Portugal, for progress and happiness for all peoples.

The three prisoners
Joao da Costa Sousa, soldier no. 51525/66 of the 1690 Company stationed at Geba (Northern Front); captured on April 10 1968 on the surrender of the colonialist garrison of Canta Cunda.
Manuel Ferreira, soldier no. 25295/65, and Augusto Dias, soldier no. 35655/66, both of the 1612 Company stationed at Buba; captured on May 20 1968 during an ambush on the Kebo/Wane road (Southern Front).

Practical problems and tactics

Text of an interview given to Tricontinental *magazine, published in issue no. 8 in September 1968*

What is that state of the struggle in the cities of so-called Portuguese Guinea, particularly in the capital, Bissao, and in Cabo Verde?

We have had a great deal of experience in the struggle in the cities and the urban centres of our country, where the struggle first began. At first we organised mass demonstrations, strikes, etc. to demand that the Portuguese change their position with regard to the legitimate rights of our people to self-determination and national independence. We found out that in the cities and urban centres the concentration of the Portuguese repressive forces—military, police, etc.—was causing us serious losses. For example, in August 1959, during the Bissao dock workers' and merchant seamen's strike, in just 20 minutes the Portuguese shot to death 50 African workers and wounded more than 100 on the Pijiguiti docks. At that time our Party decided to hold a secret conference in Bissao, and it was then that we changed direction. That is, we began to mobilise the countryside, and we decided to prepare ourselves actively for armed struggle against the Portuguese colonialist forces.

Later we decided that the Party's underground organisation would continue in the cities. The same leaders remained active in the urban centres, among them the present Party President, who, after 18 months of underground work in Bissao, was arrested by the Portuguese authorities and is still under house arrest. We decided that the popular masses in the cities should not organise any event that would give rise to criminal reprisals on the part of the Portuguese colonialists.

Today, in Bissao, Bafata, Farim, etc., our country's main urban centres, we have an underground Party organisation, but we still have not gone over to any kind of direct action against the Portuguese colonialists in the cities.

It is necessary to explain that our country is a purely commercial colony and not a colony of settlers, therefore the Portuguese civilians themselves, the *colonos,* have no great interest in establishing themselves on our lands. A few are government employees, and others are simply business-men. From the beginning they took a somewhat vacillating, if not indifferent, position on our struggle, and many of them wish to return to Portugal. Therefore, we have no reason to take action, from the standpoint of terrorism, against the Portuguese civilians. For that reason, our urban action should be aimed at the Portuguese military infrastructure and military forces. We are preparing ourselves for this, and we expect that, if the Portuguese fail to recognise our right to self-determination and independence after four years of armed struggle, we will be forced to attack in the cities also.

And we will do it, since we know that the Portuguese are determined to continue their criminal acts against our peaceful forces in the liberated areas. Thus far, we have not carried out any action in the cities, but we are determined to do so insofar as it constitutes an advance in the struggle as well as reprisal for the savage acts committed by the Portuguese against our population in the liberated areas.

As for Cabo Verde, we consider that the fight is of prime importance for the progress of our struggle not only in Guinea but in all the Portuguese colonies, and we can guarantee that our Party is getting ready to unleash armed struggle in the Cabo Verde Islands. During the past few years many political advances have been made in the Cabo Verde Islands. The Party leadership functions properly. We have excellent communication with the Cabo Verde Islands, and, as I said before, we are ready to begin armed struggle; the decision depends simply on the Party leadership, which must consider the favourable and unfavourable factors for beginning total armed struggle there.

What is the strategic aim of the armed struggle? Are there any possibilities of negotiating with Portuguese colonialism?

The strategic aim of our armed struggle of national liberation is, obviously, to completely free our country from the Portuguese colonial yoke. It is, after all, the strategic aim of all the national liberation movements, which, forced by circumstances, take up arms to fight against repression and the colonial presence. In our struggle, we established our principles after having become thoroughly familiar with our country's conditions. For instance, we decided that we should never struggle from outside and would begin the struggle within the country, for which reason we never had armed forces outside our own country. And, for the same reason, in 1963 we started the armed struggle in the centre of the country, both in the south and in the north. This means that, contrary to what has been done by other peoples in Africa or elsewhere who are fighting for national independence, we adopted a strategy that we might call centrifugal: we started in the centre and moved towards the periphery of our country. This came as the first big surprise to the Portuguese, who had stationed their troops on the

Guinea and Senegal borders on the supposition that we were going to invade our own country.

But we mobilised our people secretly, in the cities and in the countryside. We prepared our own cadres, we armed those few that we could with both traditional and modern weapons, and we initiated our action from the centre of our country.

Today the struggle is spreading to all parts of the country, in Boe and Gabu and in the south; in the north, in San Domingos, in the Farim zone; in the west, near the sea, in the Mandjakos region; and we hope to be fighting within a short time on the island of Bissao as well. Moreover, as you were able to see for yourselves in the Southern part of the country and as other newsmen and film-makers have seen in the North and East, we have liberated a large part of our national territory, which forms part of the framework of our strategy.

As to the possibilities for negotiations, we can say that our struggle seeks a political objective; we are not making war because we are militarists or because we like war. We are not making war to conquer Portugal. We are fighting because we have to in order to win back our human rights, our rights as a nation, as an African people that wants its independence. But the objectives of our war are political: the total liberation of our people of Guinea and Cabo Verde and the winning of national independence and sovereignty, both at home and on the international plane.

For this reason, it is of no importance when—today, tomorrow, or whenever—the Portuguese colonialists, forced by our armed forces, by the heroic struggle of our people, recognise that the time has come to sit down to discuss the situation with us; it does not matter when—today, tomorrow, or whenever—we are willing to enter into discussions. Therefore, the possibilities for negotiating, since the United Nations was unable to get Portugal to negotiate, depend fundamentally on the Portuguese themselves. We are also convinced that such possibilities depend on what we ourselves are able to do within the framework of our armed struggle. That is our position with regard to the possibilities of negotiating with the Portuguese; given what we have done, given the sacrifice of our people during this difficult but victorious struggle, given the fact that Africa is marching towards total independence, our position today is this: to negotiate with the Portuguese whenever they want, whenever they are ready, but to negotiate for the total and unconditional independence of our people.

That does not mean that we are not interested, as a politically aware people and in spite of the crimes committed by the Portuguese in our country, in establishing with Portugal itself the most excellent relations of collaboration and co-operation on the basis of equality, on the basis of absolute reciprocity of advantage, but likewise on the basis of the highest regard for our sovereignty.

Could you tell us something about the tactical principles followed by the PAIGC guerilla army?

At present, to carry out the armed national liberation struggle it is not necessary to invent much along general lines. Already a wealth of experience has been gained in the armed national liberation struggle throughout the world. The Chinese people fought. The Vietnamese people have been fighting for more than 25 years. The Cuban people fought heroically and defeated the reactionaries and the imperialists on their island, which is today a stronghold of progress. Other peoples have struggled and have made known to the world their experience in the struggle.

You know very well that Che Guevara, the *great* Che Guevara for us, wrote a book, a book on the guerilla struggle. This book, for example, like other documents on the guerilla struggle in other countries, including Europe, where there was also guerilla struggle during the last World War, served us as a basis of general experience for our own struggle.

But nobody commits the error, in general, of blindly applying the experience of others to his own country. To determine the tactics for the struggle in our country, we had to take into account the geographical, historical, economic, and social conditions of our own country, both in Guinea and in Cabo Verde.

It was by basing ourselves on concrete knowledge of the real situation in our country that we established the tactical and strategic principles and our guerilla struggle.

We can say that our country is very different from other countries. In the first place, it is quite a small country, about 14,000 square miles in Guinea and 1,500 square miles in Cabo Verde. While Guinea is on the African continent, Cabo Verde is in the middle of the sea, like an archipelago. We took all of this into consideration, but, in addition, Guinea is a flat country. It has no mountains, and everyone knows that in general the guerilla force uses the mountain as a starting point for the armed struggle. We had to convert our people themselves into the mountain needed for the fight in our country, and we had to take full advantage of the jungles and swamps of our country to create difficult conditions for the enemy in his confrontation with the victorious advance of our armed struggle.

111

As for our other tactics, we follow the fundamental principle of armed struggle, or, if you prefer, colonial war: the enemy, in order to control a given zone, is forced to disperse his forces; he thus becomes weakened, and we can defeat him. In order to be able to defend himself from us he needs to concentrate his forces and when he concentrates his forces he allows us to occupy the areas that are left empty and work on them politically to prevent the enemy from returning.

This is the dilemma faced by colonialism in our country, just as has been the case in other countries, and it is this dilemma, if thoroughly exploited by us, that will surely lead Portuguese colonialism to defeat in our country.

This is sure to happen, because our people are mobilised. They are aware of what they are doing. Also, the liberated regions of the country, where we are developing a new society, are a constant propaganda force for the liberation of other parts of our country.

What are the principal tactical and strategic antiguerilla principles used by the Portuguese Army?

If we have not had to invent a great deal in the course of our struggle, the Portuguese have invented even less. The only thing that the Portuguese do in our country is follow the tactics and strategies used by the US and other imperialists in their wars against the peoples who wish to free themselves of their domination. The Portuguese first attempted to work politically after having experimented with the art of repression: armed repression, police repression, murder, massacres, etc. All that did not stop the struggle. Then they tried to work politically. They exploited tribal contradictions. They even exploited racism on the basis of lighter and darker people. They exploited the question of the civilised and the uncivilised, etc., as well as the privileged position of the traditional chiefs. That did not lead to the desired results. The Portuguese then unleashed a colonial war, and in that colonial war they used the strategy and tactics that are common to all imperialists who fight against the people.

Against us, they used the most modern weapons given them by their allies, the US, Germany, Belgium, Italy, France, etc. They used every kind of bomb save the nuclear ones. In particular, they have used napalm bombs against us since the beginning of the war. They also used armoured cars. They used B-26, T-6, and P-2V planes and fighter jets—Fiat 82s, Fiat 91s, and Sabres supplied by Canada through Federal Germany, etc. None of it worked. Lately they have been using armed helicopters for combined operations with the

Navy and Infantry. We are sure that they will not work, either.

The Portuguese find themselves in the position which you have already been able to observe, since you came to our country in a way that, unfortunately, no Portuguese has done—since you came as journalists. They are closed up in their barracks; once in a while they try to make sallies to carry out criminal actions against our people. They do battle against our forces, and almost every day they bomb our villages and try to burn the crops. They are trying to terrorise our people.

We are determined to resist, and the tactics and strategies of Portuguese colonialism—which are the same as those imperialism uses, for instance, in Vietnam—just as they do not work in Vietnam, will not work in our country, either.

We know that the Portuguese carry out offensive operations using two or even three thousand men, trying to recover the already liberated territories. What can you tell us about this?

Yes, the big dream of the Portuguese has been to recover the already liberated territory. For instance, in 1964 they carried out a big offensive with almost 3,000 men against Como Island. The recovery of Como would have two advantages for the Portuguese: first, a strategic advantage, because it is a firm base for the control of the southern part of the country; secondly, a political advantage, because it would constitute a big propaganda victory for the Portuguese and would serve to demoralise our own populations.

But the Portuguese were defeated on Como, where they lost more than 900 soldiers and much material. They had to withdraw, and Como continues to be free. It is today one of the most developed zones of our liberated areas.

The Portuguese have tried and continue to try to recover ground. During the last dry season they made various efforts in both the South and the North, but they did not manage to establish themselves in either of these zones.

They come with hundreds of men—never less—and at times with thousands. It is our opinion that the more men they bring, the easier it is for us to cause them losses and damage. We are prepared to repel any attack by the Portuguese; when they advance with their aviation it is generally harder for us, but our combatants have learned from their own experience how to fight under such conditions.

Therefore, we are convinced that, whatever the number of Portuguese who come, the larger the number, the worse it will be for them; we are determined to inflict upon them ever greater defeats.

You mentioned Che Guevara's book Guerilla Warfare. **In this book Guevara divided the guerilla struggle into three phases. According to this, what phase do you think the struggle in so-called 'Portuguese' Guinea is in?**

In general, we have certain reservations about the systematisation of phenomena. In reality the phenomena don't always develop in practice according to the established schemes. We greatly admire the scheme established by Che Guevara essentially on the basis of the struggle of the Cuban people and other experiences, and we are convinced that a profound analysis of that scheme can have a certain application to our struggle. However, we are not completely certain that, in fact, the scheme is absolutely adaptable to our conditions.

With this reservation, we believe that, in the present phase of our struggle, we are already in the stage of mobile warfare. This is why we have been reorganising our forces, creating units more powerful than those of the regular army, and surrounding the Portuguese forces; this is why we have been increasing the mobility of our forces, thus diminishing the importance of the guerrilla positions in order to advance against enemy positions. But today an essential characteristic of our struggle is the systematic attacking of Portuguese fortified camps and fortresses. This in itself indicates that we are in the stage of mobile warfare. And we hope that the time is not far off when, advancing with this mobile warfare, we will at the same time have the conditions for launching a general offensive to end the Portuguese domination in our country.

Can you tell us something about the development of guerilla communications and propaganda work?

We have many difficulties in our propaganda work. First of all, thus far we do not have a radio station—which could play a role at least as important as, or more important than many guns. Our Party is actively working on getting a station so as to be able to speak daily (or, if not every day, at least several times a week) to our forces, to our people, and even to the enemy. Meanwhile, we are convinced that friendly peoples who do have stations—such as the Republic of Guinea, Senegal, Cuba, and others—will also be able to work in this area, because their broadcasts are heard in our country. They will be able to help us with broadcasts in favour of our struggle. To do so we need not issue many reports, because all are familiar with the justice and the raison d'être of our struggle.

Moreover, once in a while we communicate the results of our armed struggle. We cannot put out these communiqués with much frequency because communications are difficult between the different fronts of struggle and the centre that co-ordinates these communications (we do not as yet have an effective radio system—and we are now setting up a system of radio communication) and for that reason our communiqués at times come out after some delay. But that does not mean in the least that the struggle is not progressing in any sector. On the contrary, what happens is that our communiqués in general do not reflect the great intensity of the struggle, the frequency of the combats, and many times the victories we achieve against the enemy.

In relation to communications, our struggle has very special characteristics: we cannot fight riding in jeeps or trucks; we are the first to know that our country does not have good roads, since we ourselves have cut down the few existing bridges, we have destroyed many sections of highways, and our people have felled trees to block the highways. In fact, the enemy today can travel on almost no road in our country. Therefore, we do not have trucks, jeeps, etc., to travel along the roads that we ourselves mine. We have to move on foot within our territory. This makes communications extremely difficult.

As I said, we are working actively to improve our radio communications in such a way as not only to give daily reports on the progress of the struggle on all fronts, but also to facilitate the co-ordination of the struggle on all fronts, to make our armed struggle progress.

Can you tell us something about the difficulties met during the development of the struggle with relation to tribal and linguistic problems, difficulties with feudal chieftains in Guinea-Bissao?

The difficulties of our struggle were mainly those inherent in our situation as an underdeveloped—practically non-developed—people whose history was held back by colonialist and imperialist domination. A people that started with nothing, a people that had to begin the struggle almost naked, a people with a 99% illiteracy rate—you have already seen the effort that we have to make now to teach our people to read and write, to create schools—a people that had only 14 university-trained men—this people was surely going to have difficulties in carrying out its armed struggle.

You know that this was the situation with Africa in general, but it was very pronounced in our country. Our people were not only underfed but also the victims of many diseases because the Portuguese never concerned themselves with

115

decent public health in our land. All this caused difficulties at the beginning of the struggle.

Another difficulty is the following: our own African culture, which corresponds to the economic structure we still have, made certain aspects of the struggle difficult. These are the factors that those who judge the struggle from outside do not take into consideration but that we had to consider, because it is one thing to struggle in surroundings where everyone knows what rain, high tide, lightning, storms, typhoons, and tornadoes are, and another to fight where natural phenomena can be interpreted as a product of the will of the spirits.

That is very important for a struggle such as ours. Another difficulty is as follows: our people fought as one, opposing their traditional weapons to colonial domination at the time of the colonial conquest. But today we must wage a modern war. A guerilla war, but a modern one, with modern tactics. That also creates difficulties for us: it is necessary to create cadres, to prepare the combatants properly. Before, we had to prepare them during the struggle itself because we did not have time to build schools. Only today do we have schools for combatants as you know.

All of this created difficulties for us, that is, in training for the armed struggle. While the Portuguese officers who lead the Portuguese fight have seven years of training in military academies, in addition to the other basic courses they receive, we have to bring to the struggle young people from the cities or the countryside, some of them without any education, who have to gain in the struggle itself the necessary experience to confront the Portuguese officers. Suffice it to say that the Portuguese Government has had to change its General Staff in our country five times, and some of the chiefs of staff were even punished. This shows that after all it is not necessary to go to a military academy to fight in one's country to win a people's freedom.

As for tribal questions, our opinion on this is quite different from that of others. We believe that when the colonialists arrived in Africa the tribal structure was already in a state of disintegration due to the evolution of the economy and historical events on the African scene. Today it cannot be said that Africa is tribal. Africa still has remnants of tribalism, in particular as far as the mentality of the people is concerned, but not in the economic structure itself. Moreover, if colonialism, through its action, did anything positive at all, it was precisely to destroy a large part of the remnants of tribalism in certain parts of our country.

Therefore, we have had no great difficulties as far as tribalism is concerned. We did have trouble creating in our people a national awareness, and it is the struggle itself that is cementing that national awareness. But all the people in general, from whatever ethnic group, have been easily led to accept the idea that we are a people, a nation, that must struggle to end Portuguese domination, because we do not fall back on cliches or merely harp on the struggle against imperialism and colonialism in theoretical terms, but rather we point out concrete things. It is a struggle for schools, for hospitals, so that children won't suffer. That is our struggle. Another goal of the struggle is to present ourselves before the world as a worthy people with a personality of our own. This is the motivating force of our people. We also know that the vestiges of tribalism in our country have been eliminated through the armed struggle we are waging. Moreover we want to stress that in general the African people, both in our country and in the Congo, where terrible things took place from the tribal point of view, are not tribalist. Among the people of Africa, the tendency is to understand one another as much as possible. Only political opportunists are tribalists: individuals who even attended European universities; who frequented the cafés of Brussels, Paris, Lisbon, and other capitals; who are completely removed from the problems of their own people—they may be called tribal, these individuals who at times even look down on their own people but who, out of political ambition, take advantage of attitudes still existing in the minds of our people to try to achieve their opportunist aims, their political goals, to try to quench their thirst for power and political domination.

With regard to our country, we want to add that the armed struggle is not only wiping out the remnants of tribal ideas that might still exist but that it is also profoundly transforming our people.

You must have had the opportunity to see how, in spite of the fact that we still live in poverty, in spite of the fact that we still do not have enough clothing and our diet lacks vitamins, fresh foods, and even meat and other protein foods—all this a part of the colonial heritage and our state of underdevelopment—a great transformation is going on in many places. And you must have found the new man, the new man who is emerging in our country, the new woman who is emerging in our country. And, if you had the opportunity to speak to the children, you would see that even our schoolchildren are already politically and patriotically aware and desire the independence of our country. They have an awareness of mutual understanding, of national unity and of unity on the African continent.

We want to emphasise in particular that the women of our country are winning an independence for which so many have fought unsuccessfully. You saw, surely, how there were women in charge of the committees in the *tabancas** and the zones and even of inter-regional committees. These women are conscious of their worth and their role within our Party, and I can say that there are women on all levels of our Party.

Could you tell us briefly how the political and military leadership of the struggle is carried out?

The political and military leadership of the struggle is one: the political leadership. In our struggle we have avoided the creation of anything military. We are political people, and our Party, a political organisation, leads the struggle in the civilian political, administrative, technical, and therefore also military spheres. Our fighters are defined as armed activists. It is the Political Bureau of the Party that directs the armed struggle and the life of both the liberated and unliberated regions where we have our activists. Within the Political Bureau is a War Council composed of members of the former who direct the armed struggle. The War Council is an instrument of the Political Bureau, of the leadership of the armed struggle.

Each front has its command. On the sector level there is a sector command, and each unit of our regular army also has its command. That is the structure of our armed struggle, and it is true that the guerrillas are installed in bases and that each base has a base chief and a political commissar. In relation to organisation proper, a Party congress is generally held every two years, but within the framework of the struggle it is held whenever it is possible. The Party has a Central Committee and a Political Bureau which directly lead the local bodies—that is, the Northern and Southern inter-regional committees and the sector and *tabanka* committees. That is our structure.

In the cities and urban centres, the Party organisation remains underground, in general under the leadership of a very small number of individuals.

Since outside aid is so important to the national liberation struggle and particularly to that of Guinea-Bissao, we would like to know which countries are giving aid to your guerilla struggle.

A basic principle of our struggle is our counting on our own forces, our own sacrifices, our own efforts, but considering the characteristic underdevelopment of our people, of our country, the economic backwardness of our country, it is very difficult for us to produce weapons. Taking into account

ages.

these circumstances, taking into account the fact that in our country 99% of the people are illiterate, which makes the immediate existence of cadres difficult; and also taking into account that the enemy, which has no scruples, is aided by its NATO allies, in particular, the United States, Federal Germany, and some other countries, and above all by its South African racist allies—taking into account all this and also the essential characteristic of our times, which is the general struggle of the peoples against imperialism and the existence of a socialist camp, which is the greatest bulwark against imperialism, we accept and request aid from all the peoples that can give it to us. We do not ask for aid in manpower: there are enough of us to fight and defeat colonialism in our country. We ask for aid in weapons, in articles of prime necessity to supply our liberated regions, in medicines to heal our wounded and cure our sick and to provide medical care for the population of the liberated regions. We ask for any and all aid that any people can offer us. We also ask different countries for aid in preparing our cadres. Our aid ethics are as follows: we never ask for the aid we need. We expect that each will conscientiously give what help he can to our people in our struggle for national liberation. As part of this aid we point above all to that of Africa. Through the OAU, Africa has granted us some aid. We consider that this aid, thus far, is not sufficient to meet our needs, to provide for the development of our struggle, which is today a real war against an enemy that possesses powerful weapons to use against us and which receives aid from its allies. For example, Federal Germany even sends aviation technicians to train the Portuguese in Bissao, and, in addition, it receives Portuguese wounded for treatment in Germany to prevent the Portuguese people from seeing how many we have wounded in our country.

Our opinion is that aid from Africa is good, but insufficient. Therefore, we hope that the African peoples, the African states through the OAU can increase their aid, both financial and material.

And on the financial plane we want to point out that today our expenses are enormous. In petrol alone, we use almost 40,000 litres to supply the fighting fronts. All this involves large expenditures, and thus far we have not received the financial aid necessary to cover the costs of the war, while Portugal, in addition to its state budget, receives fabulous aid in dollars, marks, and pounds from its allies.

We want to add that within the framework of Africa there are some countries that aid us bilaterally. For example, we receive the greatest support from the Republic of Guinea, the greatest facilities for the development of our struggle. Algeria continues to help; the UAR, also. At the beginning of the struggle Morocco helped, and we don't understand why it no longer gives us the help it gave us at that time.

Other African countries have aided us. For example, Tanzania, which aids the people of Mozambique, and the Congo (Brazzaville), which aids the people of Angola, also aid us.

We want to mention the special aid given to us by the peoples of the socialist countries. We believe that this aid is a historic obligation, because we consider that our struggle also constitutes a defence of the socialist countries. And we want to say particularly that the Soviet Union, first of all, and China, Czechoslovakia, Bulgaria, and other socialist countries continue to aid us, which we consider very useful for the development of our armed struggle. We also want to lay special emphasis on the untiring efforts—sacrifices that we deeply appreciate—that the people of Cuba—a small country without great resources, one that is struggling against the blockade by the US and other imperialists—are making to give effective aid to our struggle. For us, this is a constant source of encouragement, and it also contributes to cementing more and more the solidarity between our Party and the Cuban Party, between our people and the Cuban people, a people that we consider African. And it is enough to see the historical, political, and blood ties that unite us to be able to say this. Therefore, we are very happy with the aid that the Cuban people give us, and we are sure that they will continue increasing their aid to our national liberation struggle in spite of all difficulties.

At present there is a very important problem, a burning issue in the Middle East, the Israeli aggression against the Arab peoples. What is the PAIGC's position in regard to this conflict?

We have as a basic principle the defence of just causes. We are in favour of justice, human progress, the freedom of the people. On this basis we believe that the creation of Israel, carried out by the imperialist states to maintain their domination in the Middle East, was artificial and aimed at the creation of problems in that very important region of the world. This is our position: the Jewish people have lived in different countries of the world. We lament profoundly what the Nazis did to the Jewish people, that Hitler and his lackeys destroyed almost six million during the last World War. But we do not accept that this gives them the right to occupy a part of the Arab nation. We believe that the people of Palestine have a right to their homeland. We therefore think that all the measures taken by the Arab peoples, by the Arab nation, to recover the Palestinian Arab homeland are justified.

In this conflict that is endangering world peace we are entirely in favour of and unconditionally support the Arab peoples. We do not wish for war; but we want the Arab peoples to obtain the freedom of the people of Palestine, to free the Arab nation of that element of imperialist disturbance and domination which Israel constitutes.

What is the Party's position on the struggle in Vietnam?

For us, the struggle in Vietnam is our own struggle. We consider that in Vietnam not only the fate of our own people but also that of all the peoples struggling for their national independence and sovereignty is at stake. We are in solidarity with the people of Vietnam, and we immensely admire their heroic struggle against US aggression and against the aggression of the reactionaries of the southern part of Vietnam, who are no more than the puppets of US imperialism.

We offer all our support to the people of Vietnam. Under the present historical circumstances of our people, we can do no more than fight every day with valour and determination against the Portuguese colonialists, who are also the lackeys of international imperialism.

What is your opinion of the revolutionary struggle in Latin America?

Within the framework of our firm position in favour of the peoples, we understand that the peoples of Latin America have suffered enormously. The independence of the peoples of Latin America was a sham. The peoples of Latin America never enjoyed true independence. Governments were created that were completely submissive to imperialism, in particular to US imperialism. We all know that the Monroe Doctrine was the US point of departure for the total domination of Latin America. This means that the peoples of Latin America who had been subjected to the Spanish yoke—or to that of Portugal, in Brazil, for example —passed over to the imperialist yoke in spite of having their own governments—that is, a fictitious political independence.

Today the peoples of Latin America—whose development has reached a higher level than that of the African peoples, where class contradictions are more clearly defined, and also therefore the positions of different individuals in regard to true independence—are determined, and they prove it in practice, to use whatever means are necessary to fight for their genuine national independence. We could not do less than offer the greatest support to the peoples of Latin America. We follow with a great deal of interest the development of new guerrilla *focos* in Latin America. We

121

hope that they will develop further with every passing day and that their leaders will show determination in this struggle.

We believe that each people and each leadership should be free to choose the road of struggle that best suits it, but we also expect each people and each leadership to know how to recognise when the real moment of struggle has arrived, because the enemy always fights with every means at its disposal. There will be disputes over whether or not to carry out armed struggle. Within the framework of the national liberation of the peoples there is no problem of armed or unarmed struggle. For us, there is always armed struggle. There are two kinds of armed struggle: the armed struggle in which the people fight empty-handed, unarmed, while the imperialists or the colonialists are armed and kill our people; and the armed struggle in which we prove we are not crazy by taking up arms to fight back against the criminal arms of the imperialists.

We believe that the people of Latin America have already grasped this and are showing their clearsightedness by taking up arms to fight with valour against the reactionary and imperialist forces infesting the Latin American continent.

Message to the people of Portugal

Declaration to Voz de Liberdade *radio (Khartoum January 1969)*

The Khartoum Conference marks for us a new stage in our struggle in relation to international public opinion. We have never before had a meeting of this kind, with the objective of informing the representatives of anti-colonialist opinion, particularly in Europe and America, about the advance of our struggles, about the concrete situations in our countries, and about the negative and even criminal attitude of the Portuguese colonialist government.

We are convinced that the Conference will fulfil its purpose. From now on, international public opinion, being better informed, will be able to take more concrete measures to show its solidarity with the struggle of the African peoples of the Portuguese colonies.

On the question of the freeing of prisoners-of-war by the PAIGC, I would like to say that for our people in Guinea and Cabo Verde and for our combatants in general, the freeing of three more Portuguese prisoners-of-war at Christmas does not constitute anything new, and is in line with our policy. We have always clearly proclaimed that we never confuse the people of Portugal with Portuguese colonialism. In March 1968 we freed three prisoners-of-war, and in the context of Christmas we considered it worthwhile to free three more. This gesture towards the Portuguese people also proves to the world that the Portuguese colonialist government is lying when it claims that we are bandits, terrorists and a savage people.

We expressed to the three freed prisoners our desire that they should rejoin their families and speak to them about us, so that in this way, despite the crimes of the colonialist government, the links between our people and the people of Portugal should be maintained.

Obviously when a government faces the situation in which the Portuguese government finds itself, it has to lie, and lie a lot. This we understand but can never accept.

If the war communiqués of the fascist government, in an attempt to conceal the existence of prisoners, claim that soldiers have died or disappeared and these soldiers then 'miraculously' appear, only one conclusion can be drawn from such lies, namely that the Portuguese government has no consideration either for its own people, to whom it tells gross lies, or for the young men who, at the cost of sacrifices and of their own lives, are fighting without glory in a criminal war in our country.

We consider that a prisoner-of-war deserves respect, because he is giving his life, whether or not the cause he is fighting for is just. For this reason we call on the people and patriots of Portugal to force the government to respect the people it governs and to respect the minimum of international norms regulating the situation of prisoners-of-war.

Many people thought that the political eclipse of Salazar would mean at the very least some modifications by the Portuguese government with regard to respect for international laws and above all with regard to the defence of the interests of the Portuguese people.

Salazar, whose mind was obstinately closed to the realities of the world today, carried out a policy which dragged him into the enormous pit of colonial war. But Marcelo Caetano was not obliged to fall into the same pit; his continuing of Salazar's colonial policy is conscious and truly criminal. To justify his attitude. Marcelo Caetano has to invent 'historias do arco-da-velha'*, as they say in Portugal.

The story that we are fighting in order to create in Guinea a base from which to attack Cabo Verde and hand it over to the Communists means that Marcelo Caetano thinks he can still deceive the Portuguese people. We are certain that the Portuguese people will not let themselves be deceived, and we and the patriots of Portugal are here today to put things in their proper perspective.

We are fighting to effectively liberate Guinea and Cabo Verde, in order that our peoples may have the possibility of determining their own destinies. If we took up arms to fight against Portuguese colonialism, against foreign domination in our country, it was not so that we could then hand our country over to somebody else. We repeat what we have already proclaimed many times: we want to liberate our country in order to create in it a new life of work, justice, peace and progress, in collaboration with all the peoples of the world, and most of all with the people of Portugal.

What Marcelo Caetano fears is that the Portuguese people will know that Guinea and Cabo Verde will be part of a free and independent Africa, willing to collaborate openly and loyally with the Portuguese people. While fighting for the total liberation of our country, we do not lose sight of an objective which we consider important for our own people, namely fraternal collaboration and co-operation with the people of Portugal.

*An expression peculiar to Portuguese, meaning a fairytale or long, fantastic story. Ed.

When Marcelo Caetano says that Guinea must be defended whatever the price, the price he is thinking of is the life of the young Portuguese whom he is going to send to their deaths like the many who have already been killed or mutilated. We know that the Portuguese colonialist government is going to send to our country a further 10 or 15 thousand men, or even 20 thousand as they are beginning to say. However many they send, the Portuguese government will just be sending them to their death. This is why the Portuguese people must oppose this, and demand the return of its sons who are dying for an unjust cause while their own country lacks young hands to work the land, to build Portugal and, as the poets say, to rediscover their own country.

We know (and I speak as a technician) that Portugal has the means of offering a dignified life to all its sons. That is to say that it is their own country which the Portuguese must defend and build with their efforts and sacrifices, and in a certain future they will collaborate with us of Guinea and Cabo Verde, and we will all link hands fraternally, on the basis of history, of friendship and of all the ties that unite us.

In relation to the demonstrations against the colonial wars which have recently taken place in Portugal, we must say that we appreciate them greatly and are following them very attentively. We have always said to our people, to our combatants, that the Portuguese people is a worthy people which in the course of history has already made an outstanding contribution to the evolution of humanity.

We wish to affirm to you that the attitude of the students and people in their recent demonstrations, both at the church of S. Domingos and on the occasion of the funeral of Antonio Sergio, should be a source of encouragement to you and above all a confirmation of the fact that no contradictions exist between the people of Portugal and our people, that there is not, has never been, and will never be any conflict to separate them, and that whatever crimes the colonialists may commit, in the future our people will join hands in fraternal collaboration.

Marcelo Caetano, when he took over from Salazar, could have ended the colonial wars, but did not want to. We are certain that this mission will be accomplished by the Portuguese people, by their workers and peasants, by their young people, by their progressive and anti-colonialist intellectuals, in fact by all those who truly respect and love Portugal and who know that to fight against the colonial war is to save Portugal from the suffering, ruin and danger for their own independence which this war creates.

Towards final victory

Condensed version of an interview recorded at the Khartoum Conference in January 1969, published in Tricontinental *no. 12*

An important aspect of colonialism in our country, and in other Portuguese colonies as well, is Portugal's underdevelopment; the economic, social and cultural backwardness of Portugal, which also means backwardness in the economic development of our country, backwardness in the cultural development of our people and which creates specific conditions in the political development of our country. I am not going to mention the other aspects of Portuguese colonisation, but I want to point out that while on the one hand the character of Portuguese underdevelopment permitted the European and the African to live together (which was not the case, for example, in the English colonies), on the other hand Portuguese colonials always—often through ignorance, sometimes because of misinformation, and almost always because of their need to dominate—showed a complete lack of respect and consideration for the African personality and the African culture. It is sufficient for example to look at how Europe (mainly France, Belgium and England) became full of African works of art; this opened the way to universal knowledge of the abilities of the African, of his culture in general, of his religions and philosophical concepts—in other words the way in which the African confronts the reality of the world with cosmic reality. In Portugal no such thing occurred. Either because the colonials sent to our country were generally ignorant, or because the intellectuals were never interested, the Portuguese did not know the African, even though they came from the European country with the most colonies in Africa.

Thus as a result of our struggle, as a result of our confrontation with the Portuguese, they realised that we were not what they had supposed, and they discovered an African they had never imagined. This was one of the surprises the enemy got from our struggle.

Before initiating armed struggle, we decided to create African organisations. In 1954 we began to create recreational organisations, because at that time it was impossible to give them a political character. This was important, not because of the idea of creating organisations, but because the colonialists would not allow it; this showed our youth, who had become enthusiastic with the idea, that everything was prohibited to the African under the Portuguese.

After the Party was created in 1956, there was an important moment in 1959, when the Portuguese committed the massacre of Pijiguiti, which aroused indignation among the entire population of Guinea and Cabo Verde. That was a crucial, decisive moment, because it showed that our Party was following a mistaken line and that it lacked experience. At that time the Party knew nothing of what was happening in the world, and we had to progress on an empirical basis. It wasn't until 1961 that I got to know the works of Mao Tse-Tung. Our lack of experience made us think that we could fight in the cities with strikes and so on, but we were wrong and the reality of that moment showed us that this was impossible.

In September 1959, little more than a month after the Pijiguiti massacre, we held a secret conference in Bissao which gave a completely new turn to the character of our struggle. We began to prepare ourselves for armed struggle and we decided to go into the countryside. The President of the Party, Rafael Barbosa, was the first to leave for the bush to mobilise the people and to form new party members. Our city people also went, workers, employees, etc.; they left their things and went into the bush to mobilise the population.

Later the Party decided to take advantage of the existence of independent countries, at least of one of the neighbouring independent countries. While internal factors are decisive, one cannot forget the external factors. The fact that the Republic of Guinea was next to us enabled our Party to install there, temporarily, some of our leaders, and this enabled us to create a political school to prepare political activists. This was decisive for our struggle. In 1960 we created a political school in Conakry, under very poor conditions.

Militants from the towns—Party members—were the first to come to receive political instruction and to be trained in how to mobilise our people for the struggle. After comrades from the city came peasants and youths (some even bringing their entire families) who had been mobilised by Party members. Ten, twenty, twenty-five people would come for a period of one or two months. During that period they went through an intensive education programme; we spoke to them, and night would come and we couldn't speak any more because we were completely hoarse. Some of the Party cadres would explain the situation to them, but we went further.

We performed in that school as in a theatre, imagining the

mobilisation of the people of a *tabanca,* but taking into account social characteristics, traditions, religion—all the customs of our peasant population.

In this connection, I want to make a point about the situation of our countryside. We speak of peasants, but the term 'peasant' is very vague. The peasant who fought in Algeria or China is not the peasant of our country.

It so happens that in our country the Portuguese colonialists did not expropriate the land; they allowed us to cultivate the land. They did not create agricultural companies of the European type as they did, for instance, in Angola, displacing masses of Africans in order to settle Europeans. We maintained a basic structure under colonialism—the land as co-operative property of the village, of the community. This is a very important characteristic of our peasantry, which was not directly exploited by the colonisers but was exploited through trade, through the differences between the prices and the real value of products. This is where the exploitation occurs, not in work, as happens in Angola with the hired workers and company employees. This created a special difficulty in our struggle—that of showing the peasant that he was being exploited in his own country.

Telling the people that "the land belongs to those who work on it" was not enough to mobilise them, because we have more than enough land, there is all the land we need. We had to find appropriate formulae for mobilising our peasants, instead of using terms that our people could not yet understand. We could never mobilise our people simply on the basis of the struggle against colonialism—that has no effect. To speak of the fight against imperialism is not convincing enough. Instead we use a direct language that all can understand:

"Why are you going to fight? What are you? What is your father? What has happened to your father up to now? What is the situation? Did you pay taxes? Did your father pay taxes? What have you seen from those taxes? How much do you get for your groundnuts? Have you thought about how much you will earn with your groundnuts? How much sweat has it cost your family? Which of you have been imprisoned? You are going to work on road-building: who gives you the tools? You bring the tools. Who provides your meals? You provide your meals. But who walks on the road? Who has a car? And your daughter who was raped—are you happy about that?"

In our new mobilisation we avoided all generalisations and pat phrases. We went into detail and made our people preparing for this kind of work repeat many times what they were going to say. This is an aspect which we considered of great importance, in our specific case, because we started from the concrete reality of our people. We tried to avoid having the peasants think that we were outsiders come to teach them how to do things; we put ourselves in the position of people who came to learn *with* the peasants, and in the end the peasants were discovering for themselves why things had gone badly for them. They came to understand that a tremendous amount of exploitation exists and that it is they themselves who pay for everything, even for the profits of the people living in the city. Our experience showed us that it is necessary for each people to find its own formula for mobilising for the struggle; it also showed that to integrate the peasant masses into the struggle, one must have a great deal of patience.

Our Party's policy regarding the tribal problem has produced very good results. As we conceive it, the tribe exists and it does not exist. When the Portuguese came to our country the tribal economic system was already disintegrating. Portuguese colonialism contributed further to that disintegration, although they needed to maintain some parts of the superstructure. As far as we were concerned it was not so much the economic base that led us to respect the tribal structure as a mobilising element in our struggle, but its cultural aspects, the language, the songs, the dances, etc. We would not impose on the Balantes the customs of the Fulas or the Mandingas. We defended these cultural differences with all our strength, but we also fought with all our strength all divisions on a political level.

Another aspect which we consider very important is the religious beliefs of our people. We avoid all hostility towards these religions, towards the type of relationships our people still have with nature because of their economic underdevelopment. But we have resolutely opposed anything going against human dignity. We are proud of not having forbidden our people to use fetishes, amulets and things of this sort, which we call *mezinhas*. It would have been absurd, and completely wrong, to have forbidden these. We let our people find out for themselves, through the struggle, that their fetishes are of no use. Happily, we can say today that the majority have come to realise this.

If in the beginning a combatant needed the assistance of a *mezinha,* now he might have one near but he understands— and tells the people—that the best *mezinha* is the trench. We can state that on this level the struggle has contributed to the rapid evolution of our people, and this is very important.

We established our guerilla bases before the armed struggle began. Our bases in the South were in the zones of Cobucare, Indjassan, Quinera, Gambara, Quitafene and

129

Sususa. In the North, initially, we had two or three bases. In that period, material was only brought in with great difficulty. Once inside the country, this material was looked after by some of the people in our guerilla bases.

We began by creating autonomous guerilla groups in the zones already mentioned. Each group was linked to the Party leadership. This was until the end of 1963. The struggle evolved very rapidly, much more so than we had expected. But with these groups we found that, given the complete integration of the population with the guerillas, some guerilla leaders became too autonomous—not in relation to the leadership as such (because in fact they were linked with the higher leadership of the Party), but in relation to some chiefs in the area. Then certain tendencies towards isolation developed, tendencies to disregard other groups and not to co-ordinate action. In view of this, we decided to hold our Congress in 1964, and this marked a crucial turning-point in our struggle. At this Congress we took a series of disciplinary measures, among these being the detention, trial and condemnation of certain guerilla leaders. We had to move on to collective leadership of the guerilla, under the direction of the Party committee.

We created zones and regions, each with Party committees, so that the Party leaders were at the same time the guerilla leaders. Things improved enormously; they were not perfect, but they were much better. In addition to this, we decided during the Congress to mobilise part of the guerilla forces to create regular forces, so as to extend the armed struggle to new areas. It is not necessary, in our opinion, to mobilise everyone for the armed struggle: it is enough to mobilise a reasonable proportion of the population. After that you can move on to creating regular forces and mobilise the rest.

Once our politico-military apparatus had been restructured, we organised ambushes and small attacks on the Portuguese, and other actions building up towards the present level of development of our struggle. With the creation of the regular armed forces we opened up new fronts, Gabu in the East and San Domingos and Boe in the West. At that time we still were not speaking of fronts, but of regions and zones of struggle, which corresponded to the regions and zones of the Party. Later it was possible to create the true fronts of the struggle. At first there were only the Northern and Southern fronts, but then as the struggle developed we established the Eastern front.

Our armed forces now form a section of the army within each front, and they can move to any place within the front. In the next stage we will be able to move units to any front where they may be needed.

I want to emphasise that the leadership of the struggle is the leadership of the Party. Inside the Political Bureau there is a War Council of which I am president as Secretary-General of the Party. There is no important military action in our country that does not pass through my hands. When there were fronts, sectors and units they had autonomy for normal, daily actions within certain limits, but any extensive modification, any new action, passed, and still passes through the hands of the War Council.

The commanders of the fronts execute the decisions made by the War Council. For example, the attack on the port of Bissao was planned by us, in every detail. It wasn't carried out on the planned date because of material difficulties, but it was planned by us in a meeting with all the comrades, at which we even chose the men who were to go. This gives an idea of how much our work has been centralised.

As regards the development of the struggle as a guerilla war, we consider ours as having developed like a living being, in successive stages. Often a stage was completed rapidly, sometimes slowly. We never rushed any stage: when one stage was completed, we moved on to the next. This gave an overall harmony to our struggle. At first we did not speak of an army, and even now we don't speak of a general staff. We created small guerilla groups which performed their activities, and these were tightened and tightened until they constituted an army, our regular forces.

Moving from one stage to the next, in 1967 we reached the final stage: all the guerilla forces had become regular forces. Our armed forces today consist of these regular forces and the people's armed militia, based in the liberated areas.

I want to point out that before this, our guerilla bases were actually villages, but we gradually altered this. We reduced the number of bases, joining them up in twos and threes, then we finally eliminated this type of base altogether. Now they no longer exist: there are our people's villages, and there are support points for our armed forces. The elimination of the bases was extremely fortunate, because the Portuguese had pinpointed all of them on their maps and they intended to bomb them. In fact they did bomb some, but there was no one there. We had eliminated the famous guerilla bases just in time.

The tactics of the Portuguese are those common in this kind of struggle. Once they realised that we were beating them badly, they began bombing and burning our villages, to terrorise the people and keep them from supporting us. The main concern of the enemy in this type of struggle is to deny the guerilla the support of the population. I do not think there is any need to describe in detail the tactics and strategy of the Portuguese, because they are a more or less exact copy of those used by the United States in Vietnam. The only difference is that the Portuguese do not have the same equipment as the United States.

At first the helicopters hurt us a lot, particularly their surprise attacks on our people. But now we are successfully fighting back against the helicopters; they are being downed by our guns, and the Portuguese have been forced to conclude that their helicopters cannot win the war for them.

One very important factor is that the Portuguese don't have any problems in the Cabo Verde Islands at the moment. When we begin the action there, the struggle in Guinea will be practically over. It is not an indispensable condition for the ending of the struggle, which can end without it. But the day that our action is extended to Cabo Verde, the struggle will definitely be near its end.

The past year has been filled with victories, although I do not claim that we have not suffered any setbacks—these are normal in any war. We attacked all the urban centres in our country, except Bissao—if we don't count the attacks on Bissao airport. Important centres such as Bafata, Gabu, Farim, Mansoa, Cansumbo and Bolama were attacked several times. We took a number of prisoners; there were several deserters; and we destroyed more Portuguese boats than ever before.

The sum total of our military operations from April 16th to November 15th, 1968, is as follows: 251 attacks on Portuguese fortified camps, 2 attacks on airports, 2 attacks on ports, 94 vehicles destroyed, 30 ships sunk, 4 planes downed, an estimated minimum of 900 enemy killed and 12 captured. Our armed forces made extraordinary efforts, forcing the Portuguese to evacuate some of their fortified posts. They had to evacuate Beli, in the east, Cacocoa and Sanchonha, two very important posts near the southern border, and nine other camps in the south and east of the country.

It has been a year of triumph in the political, administrative, social and cultural fields. Militarily, the struggle has reached a new stage of development and we are already capable of taking the Portuguese camps. But we are not in a hurry, we move very calmly. We have to be very careful, we have to fight according to our conditions, advancing with caution. It seems to us that it is very important now to further concentrate our action in the urban centres, to create great insecurity. We are definitely going to do this. We know that the Portuguese are going to use gas against us, but this is going to be very difficult for them. We are prepared to face every situation.

New Year's message, January 1969

Extracts from message recorded in the studios of Radio Libertacao and broadcast on January 1 1969

To the people of Guinea and Cabo Verde
To the cadres, militants and combatants of our Party
Compatriots and comrades

At the beginning of this new year of 1969, in which our armed struggle for national liberation ends its sixth year, I have great pleasure in addressing to you this message of greetings, of felicitations and of certainty of final victory for our glorious fight against the criminal Portuguese colonialists.

Our people, the cadres, militants and combatants of our great Party have good reason to celebrate the new year and the anniversary of our struggle with strengthened hope and with greater certainty of the final victory of our struggle for the independence, freedom, peace and progress of our people in Guinea and Cabo Verde.

As you all know, we started virtually from nothing. In the face of the repression and the crimes of the Portuguese colonialists we managed to organise and consolidate our Party and, step by step, to develop the armed struggle in Guinea, and we have now freed from colonial domination more than two thirds of our country and more than half our population. We are preparing for a new phase of the struggle in Cabo Verde. We are developing production, education, health facilities and trade in our liberated areas. We have made the name of our people well known in Africa and in the world. We have created and are creating hundreds of political, military, technical and scientific cadres. We guarantee, with complete certainty, the continuation of our struggle until final victory.

For six years the criminal Portuguese colonialists, with the help of their allies, have used every available means of destruction against us and have increased the strength of their troops sevenfold; they have changed their governor and commanders as we would change shirts; they have tried every sort of propaganda, lies and political intrigues to demobilise our people and our combatants; they have committed acts of aggression against neighbouring countries and have done everything possible to halt our struggle—but they have not succeeded.

On the contrary, our people is becoming more aware of its strength and our Party is growing stronger each day, our armed forces are more powerful than ever, with more com-

batants and cadres, with greater experience and more powerful weapons. This, compatriots and comrades, is the greatest
victory of our people and our great Party in these six years:
the successful continuation of our struggle, the constant
improvement of our political and military organisation, the
ever-growing certainty that no power on earth can halt the
advance of our people towards national independence. This
is also the greatest defeat for the Portuguese colonialists who
have done everything to stop our struggle but today are
forced to recognise that this is impossible.

Compatriots and comrades: those of you who have heard
or read the speech of the new head of the Portuguese
government to the National Assembly of his country will be
proud of the outstanding place given to our struggle in that
speech. In fact the new head of the criminal Portuguese
colonialists could not conceal the desperate situation of the
colonial war in our country and in his speech he had to
make propaganda for the successes and importance of our
struggle.

You will also have heard the speech made in Bissao a few
days ago by the military governor of the criminal Portuguese
colonialists. This speech too was good propaganda for our
struggle because it clearly showed the desperate situation of
the Portuguese military governor here in our country and
because it once again showed to our people and our combatants that our struggle is a just one and that we have a
right to the progress for which we are fighting. Money to
buy more traditional chiefs, salary increases for officials,
wage increases for workers, schools, hospitals, surfaced roads,
various agricultural improvements, electricity and water for
all houses, ventilator fans and refrigerators for families, etc,
etc—all this was promised by the military governor of
Bissao. Our people, whether they be in the towns or in the
countryside, know what the promises of the criminal
Portuguese colonialists are worth, but they know above all
that our dignity as an African people, our struggle, the independence we have already won in the greater part of
Guinea, cannot be bought. They know too that without our
struggle, without the great victories won by our Party, the
Portuguese military governor would not have needed to
make all these promises in order to try to deceive us and remain in our country. This is why on hearing promises of so
many good things our people in town and country will certainly have said as usual: "Djarama PAIGC—thanks to
the Party!"

At the beginning of this new year of struggle we must tell
the criminal Portuguese colonialists, loudly and clearly, that
if this is the way they want things they are going to pay
dearly, very dearly, not to *remain* here but to be *driven out*

of our country! Whatever works they hastily carry out on Bissao island or in some urban centres, whatever last-minute efforts they may make, they are surely going to be run out of our country, because our people is going to free itself completely from the odious Portuguese colonial domination and build for itself, through work in dignity and independence, a life of liberty, justice and progress for all, the main objective in the programme of our great Party.

We are going to make the year 1969—which marks the 10th anniversary of the Pijiguiti massacre—a year of decisive enlargement of the struggle, a year of even greater victories than those won previously, a year in which we will prove to the criminal Portuguese colonialists that our people does not need their consent to be a free and independent nation with its own personality in the international field.

We must mete out just punishment to the traitors among our people, those who continue to serve the criminal Portuguese colonialists against the interests of our people. We are going to show these traitors clearly that it is now time to decide: either they must cease being the servants of the Portuguese colonialists or they must be totally destroyed.

We must intensify our struggle, our political work and our military action, and bring armed struggle to every corner of our country in which there are still colonialist troops. In our political work, we are going to create more *comités de base* for the Party, increase production, improve education, health services and all the other services of our developing state. In the armed struggle we are going to use more weapons, and more powerful weapons, reinforcing the initiative and ease of movement and fire for our Popular Army, to inflict new and more crushing defeats on the criminal Portuguese colonialists.

Until the total liberation of our people in Guinea and Cabo Verde.
Forward, compatriots and comrades, in our glorious struggle for national liberation!
Long live the courageous combatants, cadres and militants of our Party!
Long live the PAIGC, strength, guide and light of our heroic people!
Death to the criminal Portuguese colonialists!

Appendix
The PAIGC Programme

I Immediate and total independence

1.Immediate winning, by all necessary means, of the total and unconditional national independence of the people of Guinea and the Cabo Verde Islands.

2.Taking over of power, in Guinea by the Guinean people, and in the Cabo Verde Islands by the people of Cabo Verde.

3.Elimination of all relationships of a colonialist and imperialist nature; ending all Portuguese and foreign prerogatives over the popular masses; revision or revocation of all agreements, treaties, alliances, concessions made by the Portuguese colonialists affecting Guinea and the Cabo Verde Islands.

4.National and international sovereignty of Guinea and the Cabo Verde Islands. Economic, political, diplomatic, military and cultural independence.

5.Permanent vigilance, based on the will of the people, to avoid or destroy all attempts of imperialism and colonialism to re-establish themselves in new forms in Guinea and the Cabo Verde Islands.

II Unity of the nation in Guinea and the Cabo Verde Islands

1.Equal rights and duties, firm unity and fraternal collaboration between citizens, whether considered as individuals, as social groups or as ethnic groups. Prohibition and elimination of all attempts to divide the people.

2.Economic, political, social and cultural unity. In Guinea this unity will take into consideration the characteristics of the various ethnic groups at the social and cultural levels, regardless of the population in these groups. In the Cabo Verde Islands, each island or group of identical and close islands will be able to have certain autonomy at the administrative level, while remaining within the framework of national unity and solidarity.

3.The return to Guinea of all émigrés who wish to return to their country. The return to the Cabo Verde Islands of all émigrés or transported workers who wish to return to their country. Free circulation for citizens throughout the national territory.

III Unity of the peoples of Guinea and the Cabo Verde Islands

1.After the winning of national independence in Guinea and the Cabo Verde Islands, unity of the peoples of these countries for the construction of a strong and progressive African nation, on the basis of suitably consulted popular will.

2.The form of unity between these two peoples to be established by their legitimate and freely elected representatives.
3.Equal rights and duties, solid unity and fraternal collaboration between Guineans and Cabo Verdians. Prohibition of all
attempts to divide these two peoples.

IV African unity

1.After the winning of national independence and on the
basis of freely manifested popular will, to struggle for the
unity of the African peoples, as a whole or by regions of
the continent, always respecting the freedom, dignity and
right to political, economic, social and cultural progress of
these peoples.
2.To struggle against any attempts at annexation or pressure
on the peoples of Guinea and the Cabo Verde Islands, on
the part of any country.
3.Defence of the political, economic, social and cultural
rights and gains of the popular masses of Guinea and the
Cabo Verde Islands is the fundamental condition for the
realisation of unity with other African peoples.

V Democratic, anti-colonialist and anti-imperialist government

1.Republican, democratic, lay, anti-colonialist and anti-
imperialist government.
2.Establishment of fundamental freedoms, respect for the
rights of man and guarantees for the exercise of these
freedoms and rights.
3.Equality of citizens before the law, without distinction of
nationality or ethnic group, sex, social origin, cultural level,
profession, position, wealth, religious belief or philosophical
conviction. Men and women will have the same status with
regard to family, work and public activities.
4.All individuals or groups of individuals who by their
action or behaviour favour imperialism, colonialism or the
destruction of the unity of the people will be deprived by
every available means of fundamental freedoms.
5.General and free elections of the organisations in power,
based on direct, secret and universal voting.
6.Total elimination of the colonial administrative structure
and establishment of a national and democratic structure
for the internal administration of the country.
7.Personal protection of all foreigners living and working in
Guinea and the Cabo Verde Islands who respect the prevail-
ing laws.

VI Economic independence, structuring the economy and developing production

1.Elimination of all relationships of a colonialist and

imperialist nature. Winning of economic independence in Guinea and the Cabo Verde Islands.

2.Planning and harmonious development of the economy. Economic activity will be governed by the principles of democratic socialism.

3.Four types of property: state, co-operative, private and personal. Natural resources, the principal means of production, of communication and social security, radio and other means of dissemination of information and culture will be considered as national property in Guinea and the Cabo Verde Islands, and will be exploited according to the needs of rapid economic development. Co-operative exploitation on the basis of free consent will cover the land and agricultural production, the production of consumer goods and artisan articles. Private exploitation will be allowed to develop according to the needs of progress, on the condition that it is useful in the rapid development of the economy of Guinea and the Cabo Verde Islands. Personal property—in particular individual consumption goods, family houses and savings resulting from work done—will be inviolable.

4.Development and modernisation of agriculture. Transformation of the system of cultivating the soil to put an end to monocultivation and the obligatory nature of the cultivation of groundnuts in Guinea, and of maize in the Cabo Verde Islands. Struggle against agricultural crises, drought, glut and famine.

5.Agrarian reform in the Cabo Verde Islands. Limitation of the extension of private rural property in order that all peasants may have enough land to cultivate. In Guinea, taking advantage of the traditional agrarian structures and creating new structures so that the exploitation of the land may benefit the maximum number of people.

6.Both in Guinea and in the Cabo Verde Islands, confiscation of the land and other goods belonging to proven enemies of the freedom of the people and of national independence.

7.Development of industry and commerce along modern lines. Progressive establishment of state commercial and industrial enterprises. Development of African crafts. State control of foreign commerce and co-ordination of internal trade. Adjustment and stabilisation of prices. Elimination of speculation and unfair profits. Harmony between the economic activities of town and countryside.

8.Budgetary balance. Creation of a new fiscal system. Creation of a national currency, stabilised and free from inflation.

VII Justice and progress for all

a. On the social level

1.Progressive elimination of exploitation of man by man, of all forms of subordination of the human individual to degrading interests, to the profit of individuals, groups or classes. Elimination of poverty, ignorance, fear, prostitution and alcoholism.

2.Protection of the rights of workers and guaranteed employment for all those capable of work. Abolition of forced labour in Guinea and of the exporting of forced or 'contract' labour from the Cabo Verde Islands.

3.Fair salaries and appointments on the basis of equal pay for equal work. Positive emulation in work. Limitation of daily working hours according to the needs of progress and the interests of the workers. Progressive elimination of the differences existing between workers in the towns and those in the countryside.

4.Trade union freedoms and guarantees for their effective exercise. Effective participation and creative initiative of the popular masses at every level of the nation's leadership. Encouragement and support for mass organisations in the countryside and in the towns, mainly those for women, young people and students.

5.Social assistance for all citizens who need it for reasons beyond their control, because of unemployment, disability or sickness. All public health and hygiene organisations will be run or controlled by the state.

6.Creation of welfare organisations connected with productive activity. Protection of pregnant women and children. Protection of old people. Rest, recreation and culture for all workers, manual, intellectual and agricultural.

7.Assistance for victims of the national liberation struggle and their families.

b. On the level of education and culture

1.Teaching centres and technical institutes will be considered as national property and as such run or controlled by the state. Reform of teaching, development of secondary and technical education, creation of university education and scientific and technical institutes.

2.Rapid elimination of illiteracy. Obligatory and free primary education. Urgent training and perfection of technical and professional cadres.

3.Total elimination of the complexes created by colonialism, and of the consequences of colonialist culture and exploitation.

4.In Guinea development of autochthonous languages and of the Creole dialect, creation of a written form for these languages. In Cabo Verde development of a written form for the Creole dialect. Development of the cultures of the various ethnic groups and of the Cabo Verde people. Protection and development of national literature and arts.

5.Utilisation of all the values and advances of human and universal culture in the service of the progress of the peoples of Guinea and Cabo Verde. Contribution by the culture of these peoples to the progress of humanity in general.

6.Support and development of physical education and sport for all citizens of Guinea and the Cabo Verde Islands. Creation of institutions for physical education and sport.

7.Religious freedom: freedom to have or not to have a religion. Protection of churches and mosques, of holy places and objects, of legal religious institutions. National independence for religious professionals.

VIII Effective national defence linked to the people

1.Creation of the necessary means of effective national defence: army, navy and air force, linked to the people and directed by national citizens. Those fighting for independence will form the nucleus of national defence.

2.Democratic government within the armed forces. Discipline. Close collaboration between the armed forces and the political leadership.

3.The whole people will have to participate in vigilance and defence against colonialism, imperialism and the enemies of its unity and progress.

4.Complete ban on foreign military bases on the national territory.

IX Proper international policy in the interests of the nation, of Africa and of the peace and progress of humanity

1.Peaceful collaboration with all the peoples of the world, on the basis of principles of mutual respect, national soverereignty, territorial integrity, non-aggression and non-interference in internal affairs, equality and reciprocity of advantages, and peaceful co-existence. Development of economic and cultural relations with all peoples whose governments accept and respect these principles.

2.Respect of the principles of the United Nations Charter.

3.Non-adhesion to military blocs.

4.Protection for Guinean and Cabo Verdian nationals resident abroad.

Index

Other Stage 1 books

Already published

Fidel Castro
Major Speeches
eight important recent speeches
15/-

Che Guevara
Socialism and Man in Cuba
with four other texts
5/-

Forthcoming publications

E. Cerquetti
What is NATO?
a detailed analysis of the workings of NATO and other
interlinking organisations set up to "contain Communism"

Soviets in Saclay?

Flins, the struggle of a factory
documents of industrial actions in France in 1968

Douglas Bravo
The Guerilla War in Venezuela

P. J. Cannebrava
Militarism and Imperialism in Brazil

The Congo of Lumumba and Mulele

*For regular information about these and other publications
just send your name and address to:
Stage 1, 21 Theobalds Road, London WC1*